Tennis, Drugs, and Jesus Christ

The Eric Miller True Story

by

Eric Miller

DORRANCE
PUBLISHING CO
EST. 1920
PITTSBURGH, PENNSYLVANIA 15238

The opinions expressed herein are those of the author, who assumes complete and sole responsibility for them, and do not necessarily represent the views of the publisher or its agents.

All Rights Reserved
Copyright © 2023 by Eric Miller

No part of this book may be reproduced or transmitted, downloaded, distributed, reverse engineered, or stored in or introduced into any information storage and retrieval system, in any form or by any means, including photocopying and recording, whether electronic or mechanical, now known or hereinafter invented without permission in writing from the publisher.

Dorrance Publishing Co
585 Alpha Drive
Suite 103
Pittsburgh, PA 15238
Visit our website at www.dorrancebookstore.com

ISBN: 979-8-8852-7114-1
eISBN: 979-8-8852-7841-6

Table of Contents

Chapter One — *Bloody Sheets* *1*

Chapter Two — *1969 The Frank Miller Tennis Camp* *7*

Chapter Three — *Jennifer Miller* *11*

Chapter Four — *1977 Norman Oklahoma / The Tennis Boom* . . . *15*

Chapter Five — *1980 Atheism vs Christianity* *23*

Chapter Six — *1982 My First Drink / Burning Down the House* . . *27*

Chapter Seven — *1983 Frank and Mary's Marriage /*
Craig's Relaxing Vacation to New Orleans . . *31*

Chapter Eight — *1984 Frank and Mary's Divorce /*
The Drugstore Bandit *39*

Chapter Nine — *1985 Angry Young Man /*
Steppenwolf and The Guess Who *43*

Chapter Ten — *1986 College Tennis Ada, Oklahoma /*
The Big Weed Bust *51*

Chapter Eleven — *1990 Depeche Mode Violator Tour /*
College Tennis Head Coach /
Craig Visits the Nut House *59*

Chapter Twelve — *1994 The Oklahoma City Tennis Business* . . . *67*

Chapter Thirteen — *1997 Frank Miller Dies /*
Madness in Mexico City *71*

Chapter Fourteen — *1998 Jennifer Miller Starts Drug Overdosing / The Tennis Pro Am* 79

Chapter Fifteen — *2000 The New Millennium / The Bank Robbery* 83

Chapter Sixteen — *2001 September 11th – 911 / Eric Visits the Nut House* 87

Chapter Seventeen — *2004 Living in the Woods with the Devil* .. 93

Chapter Eighteen — *2005 New Life / Men's Sober Living Home* .. 97

Chapter Nineteen — *The Insanity of Drug and Alcohol Abuse* 101

Chapter Twenty — *2007 The End of a Great Junior Tennis Program* 105

Chapter Twenty-One — *The Ghetto Tennis Courts in OKC, Oklahoma* 109

Chapter Twenty-Two — *2007 Death of Jennifer Miller / My Encounters with Famous Pro Tennis Players* 111

Chapter Twenty-Three — *2010 Switching Addictions / Madman Comedy the Frisky and Grumpy Show* 115

Chapter Twenty-Four — *2015 Suboxone Drug Treatment in OKC, Oklahoma / Mary Miller Dies* ... 121

Chapter Twenty-Five — *2017 Estes Park, Colorado / Summer in Jail* 125

Chapter Twenty-Six — *2018 to 2021 Estes Park Colorado a Test from God* 131

Chapter One

Bloody Sheets

Vindicate me, O God, and plead my cause against an ungodly nation. Oh, deliver me from the deceitful and unjust man!
—Psalm 43:1

-Tears on my Pillow, Little Anthony and the Imperials.

The Early Days of My Parents' Upbringing

My mom, Mary Miller, was born in Toledo Ohio in 1939. She had the worst life possible for a little girl. Mary was raped repeatedly by her evil alcoholic father. Her mother was a codependent. She never tried to stop the abuse and told Mary to never talk about it. Mary's brother Carey was horribly beaten by their evil father. Carey would wake up in the mornings in bloody sheets. To deal with Mary's abuse, she started drinking alcohol at a young age. Mary tried to have a normal life. She made good grades and was heavily involved in church. If I could go back in time. I would have murdered Mary's evil dad before any of the abuse started. There would be a lot more about Mary's childhood in my book. But Mary didn't want to talk about it. *"Speedoo," by The Cadilacs.*

This song reminds me of my dad growing up. My dad, Frank Miller, was born in Romney West Virginia in 1936. My dad grew up in Romney with his dad Sylvester. Sylvester was six foot four and very strong. Back then if you were six foot four you were extremely big. Sylvester fought on the front lines in World War I. Franks mom, Golda, was a great mother to the Miller kids. Franks brothers were Bill, Jim, Foster, and his sister Norene. They all had to work the farm and go to school. Back in that time, lives were a lot harder than today. I love you Uncle Bill. Roberta Bobby Miller, you're the queen of the Millers. Cousin Jimmy, you're a warrior. I'm coming to our next Miller family reunion. And I'm coming to get down.

One day the county fair came to town. There was a wrestler that would fight anyone. If you could last a couple rounds you won money. Big bad Sylvester Miller stepped up to the ring ready for war. Sylvester didn't just last a couple of rounds; he embarrassed the wrestler. Then the promoter asked my grandfather if he would take the wrestlers place and tour around with the fair. Sylvester turned it down; he was too busy with five kids and a farm.

Frank and his brother Bill were mischievous little boys. They would go running around the mountains mixing it up with nature. One day they went to the top of a mountain. The mountain was on one side of the main street in Romney. There was a huge boulder they were trying to unwedge. After a bunch of attempts the boulder flew down the mountain. The boulder blasted across the main street. It almost hit a car driving by. Somebody saw little Frank and Bill running away like wild dogs. That person told Sylvester and they were hiding from him all day. Frank and Bill feared their dad; they were planning to run away. They finally got hungry and came home that night to face the legend of Sylvester Miller.

SYLVESTER MILLER
WWI 1918

Frank and His Brother Bill Later in High School

They would take their dads car and go racing moonshiners. Frank told me you could see the moonshiner's fires in the mountains at night. Frank loved football; he started for Romney High at running back. Romney High had such a small team that Frank also played defense. Frank graduated from Romney High in 1953.

Before Frank went to college he enlisted in the Korean War. That was the only way he could pay for college. He was in boot camp in the jungles of Panama during the Korean War. I remember Frank telling me there were snakes crawling everywhere. One night a big snake crawled into a dude's sleeping bag and slept with him all night. After that some guys in Frank's company slept in the muddy road. They were trying to get away from the snakes. One of those guys was run over by a jeep. It was so muddy that night. The guy was pushed down in the mud and didn't get hurt. To get ready for war, Frank's company would break up into two different teams and play war games. Planes would drop bags of flower over the jungle acting like bombs. If you were hit by flower you had to play dead. Frank was blasted with flower; he was pure white. Frank was playing dead while the other guys were laughing. One day in bootcamp something horrible happened. Franks drill sergeant was showing Franks company how to throw a live grenade. One guy pulled the pin and dropped the grenade right in front of everyone. The drill sergeant put his helmet on the grenade with his body on top. The drill sergeant was blown up and obviously killed. He saved every one's life in my dad's company. Thank God the Korean War ended right before Frank had to go.

The government paid for Frank's college. Frank got his bachelor's degree and his master's degree in Psychology from the University of West Virginia in Morgantown. That's where he and Mary met. Mary was going to school their also. They were married in Morgantown then Craig Miller was born there in 1961. Frank moved the family to Iowa City, Iowa. Frank got another master's degree at the University of Iowa. Susan Miller was born in 1963 and I was born in 1966 in Iowa City. We lived in married housing across the street from the Hawkeyes football stadium. Frank moved us to Vermillion, South Dakota. Frank was getting his PhD in psychology and teaching psychology at the University of South Dakota, the land of Coyote football. Jennifer Miller was born in Vermillion in 1967, the summer of love. Frank moved us to Galveston, Texas for one year where Frank finished his doctorate in clinical child psychology at the hospital. Frank moved us back to Vermillion. He was teaching psychology full time at USD.

Chapter Two

1969 The Frank Miller Tennis Camp

Make a joyful shout to the Lord, all you land.

—Psalm 100:1

–Light My Fire, The Doors

In my book I'm calling marijuana, weed. It's easier to spell than marijuana.

When Frank Miller moved us to Vermillion, South Dakota we moved into a cool scary house. We moved into an old fire station house across the street from USD. This house had three floors and a spiral staircase. In the middle of the spiral staircase there was a fireman's pole. We used to slide down the fireman's pole constantly. On the first floor in our living room there was a massive mirror that covered a whole wall. The mirror scared the crap out of us kids. At night we thought our reflections in the mirror were ghosts. We had Frank take the mirror out of the house. The third floor had two big areas with a lot of twin beds. Thats where the firemen slept; it was creepy. I would love to have that house today.

In 1969 Frank and Mary loved to party and discovered weed. Frank and Mary both smoked cigarettes. Frank and Mary would have groovy late 60s parties. At the party, after Frank sent the kids to bed, I would smell something funny that wasn't cigarettes. Frank started playing tennis in college and picked the sport up fast. Frank found us places to practice tennis in the winters of South Dakota like gyms, racquetball courts, and in our house. Frank would have us hitting volleys and short court in our living room.

One day in early spring in 1972, there were six inches of snow on the USD varsity tennis courts. Frank took the whole family and a couple of snow shovels. It took us forever to shovel off the snow on two courts. We had the best time in the world playing tennis all day. As a hyperactive monkey boy, I loved doing anything physical. Tennis was a godsend and heaven on earth. That spring Frank Miller played in the Vermillion men's open singles tournament. The tournament was held at the USD tennis courts. Frank won the tournament. Watching Frank play in the tournament was amazing; he was like superman to me.

It's finally summertime in Vermillion South Dakota. It's time for the Frank Miller tennis camp. Frank would round up the kids and we played all day. Back then we were playing with wood tennis racquets. Frank would take a wooden tennis racquet and saw off the grip. Jennifer and I have little wooden junior tennis racquets. Craig and Susan did well in the South Dakota junior tennis tournaments. Jennifer and I were too young at the time for tournaments. Every day after the Frank Miller tennis camp, the Millers would attack the Vermillion public swimming pool. One day at the pool, Craig was sneaking around on the roof. He was trying to see the girls naked in the showers. Craig ran into a wasp's nest and fell of the roof. Craig was a sneaky little dude back then. Every day Craig would come home either in trouble or injured.

The coolest thing besides playing tennis for me was Cub Scouts. In the pinewood derby you were supposed to make your own car with help from your parents. Frank was so competitive he made my car by himself. Frank's car won the Vermillion pinewood derby title and went to state. Frank's car didn't place in the top three for a trophy. The next year Frank was obsessed to win state. He made my car like a mad scientist down in our basement. This time Frank's car won the Vermillion title and placed third at state. Frank let me have his third-place trophy.

Punt, Pass, and Kick came to Vermillion every year. Frank would help us practice hard on those three things. This time Frank couldn't punt, pass, and kick the ball for us. Craig got second place every year. The guy that won first-place every year went to the University of Nebraska later in life. He started at punting and kicking for the Cornhuskers. The best I ever placed in Punt, Pass, and Kick was third. The trophies looked like an Oscar with a football helmet.

Christmas time at the Miller house was magical. Just like a lot of parents they told us Santa Clause was real. One Christmas Eve, while we were sleeping, I smelt that funny smell again. Craig runs downstairs and I follow. We caught Mom getting high with Santa Clause by the Christmas tree. After that we knew Santa Clause wasn't real. He just loved to smoke weed.

All I can say about our upbringing, is that it was the opposite from my parents. My parents broke the cycle of abuse and treated us great. In the mid-70s Mary was deeply involved in the Equal Rights Amendment Movement. She had ERA meetings at our house with around fifteen female feminists sitting in a big circle. One night before a meeting, Mary told Frank to get the boys out of the house. Most of the women in the group didn't like men. That night Frank, Craig, and I came home early. All the salty women gave us a look like they wanted to wrestle us. Mary told the men to go downstairs. That was cool—women were telling men what to do. Mary was a strong, educated, and an independent woman.

Frank and Mary taught us to treat everyone equally. That was rare back in the mid-70s. We were good friends with African Americans and American Indians. My parents also taught us women are equal to men. My parents hated racism, hate, and child abuse. My parents killed the abuse and racism of their parents' generation. Thank you Mom and Dad. For breaking the cycle of abuse, racism, and treating women like objects. Education is the key, and my parents were extremely educated. My parents only flaw was drinking too much alcohol and getting high around us kids.

Chapter Three

Jennifer Miller

He will wipe every tear from their eyes. There will be no more death or mourning or crying or pain, for the old order of things has passed away.

—Revelation 21:4

-She, The Misfits

Jennifer Miller was raped in 1975 in third grade by one of the town bullies in Vermillion, South Dakota. Jennifer never said a word about her rape until she was thirty years old when she first got sober. Growing up Jennifer was always screaming and crying. Frank and Mary couldn't calm her down. It was a serious problem.

The Miller's moved to Norman, Oklahoma in the summer of 1977. Jennifer was ranked extremely high in Oklahoma ten and under tennis. Jennifer and I were in the fifth grade together because I was held back. Frank and Mary both smoked cigarettes, weed, and drank alcohol.

They didn't care if we did the same. When parents are using drugs like tobacco, weed, and alcohol it's hard to tell your children they can't use them. Kids follow examples from their parents. Like father like son or mother like daughter. Jennifer and

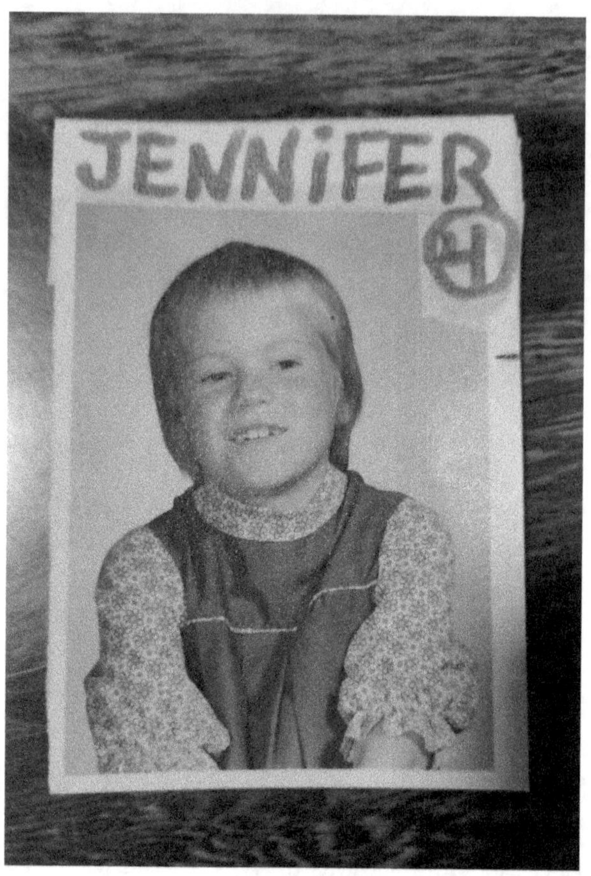

Craig were smoking cigarettes and using drugs at a really young age. They were hanging out with the wild kids in town. Jennifer was already on the fast track to self-destruction.

In sixth grade at Whittier Middle School in Norman, Jennifer already had a reputation as being a hoodlum. Trust me, nobody messed with Jennifer and her friends. By the seventh grade Jennifer was cutting on herself. Cutting on yourself means that you literally cut your skin. You're using a sharp object like a knife. One day at Whittier Middle School, Jennifer carved into her skin the word *death* with an ink pen and bleeding. Jennifer Miller was a tormented little girl. She was burning inside.

My parents went in the opposite direction from their parents' abuse. Instead of abusing the hell out of us, our parents didn't discipline us at all. We did whatever we wanted; we were like a pack of wild dogs. During that time Jennifer and I got into a bad fight. I smelled weed coming from her room. When Jennifer and her friend went outside, I found a bag of weed in her dresser and flushed it. She went crazy and smashed my wood Jack Kramer tennis racquet. I hate admitting this, but I punched her in the nose.

After that Jennifer and her older girlfriend ran away. My Mom and Dad went to the police and reported Jennifer missing. Frank and Craig went to all of Jennifer's party houses looking for her. They scared the crap out of Jennifer's older guy friends. No one knew where Jennifer was. She was gone a long time; we thought she was dead. A year later Jennifer walked in the door like nothing happened. She and her older friend went hitch hiking all over the US. The way they survived was that Jennifer's older friend would have sex with truckers for food and drugs. I apologized to Jennifer for hitting her. She told me that's not why she ran away. She wanted to party and travel. Jennifer Miller was only twelve years old.

Chapter Four

1977 Norman Oklahoma / The Tennis Boom

Those who listen to instruction will prosper, those who trust the lord will be joyful.

—Psalm 16:11

–I Feel Love, Donna Summer

That last chapter was depressing, let's have some fun. In the hot summer of 1977, the Millers moved to Norman, Oklahoma. Frank took a job at Children's Hospital in Oklahoma City. He was a clinical child psychologist. He was the head of the child psychology unit at Children's Hospital. Frank moved us to Norman instead of Oklahoma City (OKC). He loved OU football and Norman is a great place to raise children. That summer we played in a ton of Oklahoma junior tennis tournaments. Frank, Mary, and Craig would drive us to the tournaments in our 1972 Buick station wagon. Every tournament was massive; it was in the tennis boom. Back then each age division had 128 or less in every draw. If you won a couple rounds you were good. If you won the tournament, you were lethal.

That summer there was a racquet club on the east side of Norman. Club Red was paradise. The Millers hardly ever played on an indoor tennis court. Club Red had it all; a pool, indoor and outdoor courts. Back then there were men's and women's money tennis tournaments. College and pro players would come from all over the country to play. Club Red had a money tournament that summer. I couldn't believe how many great players were in the draw.

The pro that stood out the most was an Australian from Oklahoma City. Aussie OKC was great friends with the Aussie director of tennis at Club Red. Aussie OKC was ranked like sixtieth in the world. Then he came to OKC to teach tennis. Aussie OKC grew up playing against and was friends with one of the most famous Australian playing pros ever. He was the Aussie with the legendary mustache. Aussie OKC also dated the famous playing pros sister. Aussie OKC became a legend in the Oklahoma tennis scene.

Craig was a long-haired weightlifting hippy that looked like Tarzan. Susan was an all-around great girl that hated the Miller Highlife. Jennifer and I were too young for the Miller Highlife. Craig and Susan would run Franks tennis camp during the day. We were cussing, fighting, and playing all-day long. Frank put a tennis chart on our wall in the kitchen. It had all the strokes in tennis on it. We marked how many of each stroke we hit that day. When Frank came home from work, he would check out the chart. Then the Millers would hit the courts again. Everywhere the Millers were practicing tennis. People would stare at us in shock. When we were practicing, and someone told us to be quiet, the Miller's would tell that person to go *blank* themselves. The Millers were like a pack of hyenas on the tennis court. Frank tried to get us to stop cussing. He put a cussing jar in the kitchen. If the kids cussed, we had to put a quarter in the jar. If Frank or Mary cussed, they had to put a dollar in the jar. Not only did it not work, but someone always stole the money out of the jar.

Frank didn't make much money as a child psychologist with four kids. We couldn't afford tennis lessons. We bought our clothes at thrift stores. I remember having one tennis racquet at

FeeL my PAiN
SucKER!
FRANK 1977. ⑤

tournaments while the other kids had so much equipment they looked like pros. Frank would buy tennis instruction books and teach us how to play. That fall in fifth grade at Monroe elementary school was my second try at fifth grade. Jennifer and I are now in the fifth grade together. Craig is a junior at Norman High. Susan is a freshman at West Mid High.

At Monroe elementary school in fifth grade, I met a cool kid that played tennis named MF. MF and I became doubles partners in boys twelve and under. We had to play the same two big boys, in the semis or the finals, a couple times. One of them was a big red-haired boy from Shawnee. The other boy was from OKC and he's in my book in 1985, from when Casady High played Norman High. Back then Frank would take us to the record store. He would let each of us pick out an album. There would be days when Frank would go to the record store by himself. One day he brought home a Kurtis Blow record with Kurtis Blows song, "The Breaks." One day, at Whittier Middle School, my teacher let me rap the lyrics to "The Breaks" for the whole class.

Here's the Miller's average dinner back in the day. We had hamburgers, french-fries, glass quarts of Dr Pepper, and Coke, with Edger Winter's "Frankenstein" playing in the background. We ate like the Simpsons fighting over the last french fry. Our house always smelled like cigarettes and weed. I wouldn't bring my friends over because of the smell and what could be lying around, like Craig's red bong, nasty ashtrays, and beer cans. Craig would always spit his chewing tobacco in an empty glass quart bottle. One day I thought it was Dr Pepper and accidentally took a drink.

One day at Whittier in sixth grade, I was minding my own business. A kid comes up to me and wants to fight. I tell him lets meet after school out front. I'm waiting for this kid in front of Whittier. The kid is nowhere to be found and a big cocky kid shows up in his place. I tell him my fight isn't with you, let's become friends. He agreed with me and we became friends. We went to his house while a huge crowd of kids were chanting fight. We ate ham sandwiches and played ping pong. Cocky and I became great friends until this very day. At Whittier Middle School I was in special ED classes because of my learning disability. Because of that a lot of kids were calling me retarded, idiot, stupid, and more. That's why I got into a lot of fights in school. It never stopped; I was called those names my whole life.

In 1979 at Norman High, Craig and his friends were long-haired, vicious hippies. Craig and his friends were all big dudes that loved drinking and fighting. Their favorite band was Lynyrd Skynyrd. In 1979 Craig was number one on Norman High's tennis team. He broke more tennis racquets than anyone in the world. He would smash them on the court or throw them. After high school, Craig got a scholarship to play tennis for the University of Nebraska. That fall at Nebraska he was beating most of the team. Nebraska men's tennis were on a road trip. Craig was caught smoking weed in a hotel with the number one player. It probably looked like a scene in a Cheech and Chong movie. Nebraska's coach came in the room and asked whose weed is that. Craig admitted it and was kicked off the team. He came back to Norman, Oklahoma to live with us on Poplar Lane.

Frank Miller was a crazy tennis parent. He would try to coach us while we were playing in tennis tournaments. Parents coaching in tournaments is against the rules. In one Oklahoma junior tournament in boys' fourteens, Frank was telling me to hit it to his backhand constantly. The kid's mom told the tournament director. Frank got a warning and was quiet for a couple seconds. Frank kept telling me to hit it to his backhand. The tournament director told Frank to stop coaching or he was gone. Frank couldn't stop and was kicked off the sight. I watched Frank drive to the other side of the park. I watched him sneak into the bushes on the side of the court. Frank was in the bushes quietly saying hit it to his backhand. It got louder and louder; by then I lost the match.

When we got in the car I was yelling at Frank. Then Frank tells me that I should have hit it to his backhand. I went with Franks madness, and we started laughing. Because of my short attention span, I never got mad about losing in tennis and moved on to the next thing.

I started to hate junior tennis tournaments. I was tired of kids cheating and crazy tennis parents. I asked Frank if I could play in the adult tournaments with him and Craig. I started playing all the adult tournaments. I entered in the lower divisions and did well. There were no crazy tennis parents and juniors cheating. Frank was playing at the same time. He couldn't tell me to hit it to the backhand anymore. Adults were fun to play against; I never went back to juniors at age fourteen. I practiced with Frank and Craig during the week. They were the best practice partners possible. I started loving tennis again.

This is how big tennis was in the Tennis Boom: You had to wait about an hour to get a court at night. One night, Craig and I were going to Timberdale Courts. Like always, Craig would smoke a joint on the way there. Craig didn't know what it was like not to be high playing tennis. That night we didn't want to wait for a court. We went up to the two best player's court. We asked them to play doubles. We played them forever; it was awesome. It was fun playing with my big brother in doubles. We started playing men's doubles tournaments.

I loved our massive heavy Prince ball machine. I hit a million balls of it and used it as a weapon. I would put it in the garage with the door open and plug it in. I would put it on the highest speed and blast cars driving by. I had so many angry people pounding on the front door on Poplar Lane. It was great until I blasted a Norman police car. The police officer was pounding on the door. The police officer wasn't going away. I opened the door and admitted to it. The cop wasn't mad and had never seen a ball machine before. He told me not to do it again. I just didn't hit cop cars anymore. When our parents were at work we would have tennis ball wars in the house. We were hitting balls at each other with our tennis racquets. I would go upstairs and plug in the Prince ball machine. I would blast everyone downstairs. Craig was able to run upstairs and take me out. When Frank and Mary came home from work the house was destroyed, and Mary was mad. Frank was never mad; he would always ask who won.

Chapter Five

1980 Atheism vs Christianity

God is finally in the house, Amen.

—Eric Miller

–Living In Your Own Private Idaho, The B-52's

The Miller family started going in the wrong direction in life. Jennifer was already smoking cigarettes and weed. Frank and Mary let us do whatever we wanted. One day Frank told our family we were Atheist. He told us we were too smart to believe in Jesus Christ. I have anxiety, bipolar disorder, and ADHD. I was searching for something to take it all away. I wanted the opposite of the way our family lived. To me it meant searching out God and becoming a Christian. The Millers weren't the Antichrist, we were just out of control. A friend of mine, MJ, wanted God in his life also. We started going to Saint Stevens Methodist Church in Norman.

We were baptized on a Sunday. MJ's whole family was there. The Millers didn't show. That's okay, it just fueled my fire. I declared holy war on the Miller family, my preaching was relentless. I came at my family like a honey badger going for a piece of raw meat. I told them they were all going to hell. Of course, they thought it was funny. The Millers were entertained for years. I started bugging Craig worse than anyone. He and his friends were an easy target. They would go up to his room for late night bong sessions. In a creepy voice I would tell them they were all going to hell. Imagine a room full of long-haired hippies, higher than a madman, hearing that. They gave me the nickname Devil Boy.

After a year of preaching to Craig and his friends it started getting to Craig in a great way. One day Craig came up to me. He asked about Jesus Christ and he was deadly serious. I told him to go to my pastor's house down the street. Craig did it and he got a bible and was baptized. During that time my friend MJ was curious about tennis. He bought a book on how to play tennis. Just by reading the book MJ taught himself how to play. Within five years MJ was close to my level of play. MJ got better faster in tennis than anybody I've ever seen.

In 1981 it was Susan's senior year. She was playing tennis for Norman High. After Norman High, Susan left the Miller home ASAP. Susan and I were a lot alike when it came to the Miller Highlife. Some of my friends' parents wouldn't let them hang out with me. It sucks not being able to hang out with friends because of our family's reputation.

A Typical Night with the Millers on Poplar Lane

Upstairs was the hallucination zone. Jennifer and her friends would be in her room partying. Craig and his friends would be doing the same. Pretty soon the two groups would merge for a small party. My parents would be in their room drinking and getting high. Every once in a while the doorbell would ring. The number one tennis player for OU men's tennis was buying weed from Craig. While the whole Miller family is partying upstairs, I'm in my room listening to my parents threating to divorce. Now God's in my room every night with me. God is hearing me and calming me down.

TOP LEFT—SUSAN/CRAIG
Bottom LEFT—DevilBoy/Jenny
6

Chapter Six

1982 My First Drink / Burning Down the House

God makes it very clear, don't worship anything but God.
—Eric Miller

–Burning Down the House, Talking Heads

In 1982 I was a freshman at West Mid High. One night, a couple days before Christmas, Craig and Jennifer had a small party on Poplar Lane. I took my first drink that night. Right after my first drink of alcohol I was telling myself that alcohol was the greatest thing in the world. Thirty minutes later I was drinking alcohol like I was on the tennis court in the heat. I chugged a lethal amount of Jack Daniels. I took off all my clothes and went streaking around my neighborhood. I finally came home and tackled the Christmas tree. I broke a bunch of presents and passed out under the tree. Mary came downstairs pissed off, yelling at everyone. Mary knew that was my first drink. Mary helped me to my bed while I was puking my guts out. At eight AM Frank makes Craig and I play tennis at Varsity courts. Frank made us play for a couple of hours to teach us a lesson. I was puking all over the court, it didn't teach me squat. I finally went with the Miller Highlife. With my ADHD, bipolar disorder, and anxiety it terrorized me for all my young and adult life. Discovering alcohol was life changing, I could finally relax. Alcohol was better than God. Now I worship drugs and alcohol.

In 1982, I was running cross country and playing tennis for varsity at Norman High. Running cross country and playing tennis helped my anxiety. I was always listening to the B-52's on my Walkman tape player while I was running. One of the reasons I ran so much was for the runner's high. Runner's high was euphoric and relaxing; I was addicted to it. Norman High's cross-country coach made the team run eight miles every day. I would run ten miles every day chasing the runner's high. This is what the runners high felt like: I would run for a few miles feeling pain. All the sudden, I was in a dream state, flying down the road. Before I knew it, my ten-mile run was over and I was having the best trip of my life. Tennis also did that for me to a certain extent. During that time, I was a serial ringing and running machine. I loved the excitement and the challenge. I had a couple men in my neighborhood wanting to rip my head off. None of those furious men could catch me. Frank and Craig were the two baddest men on the block.

There was one dad on my block that hated me more than anyone. He wanted to catch me bad. This guy was a high ranked officer in the Army and jogged a lot. One night I set a trap for Army Man between two fences. I wove a bunch of string like a big spider web. I knew where the bottom of the trap was. I rang Army Man's doorbell a couple times. He exploded out of his door in a furious rage. I purposely ran down to the string trap. I ran under the string trap. Army Man doesn't. This trap worked perfectly. It stopped Army Man dead in his tracks.

I ran home and locked my front door. Army Man comes pounding on the door at Poplar Lane. Frank is asking me what I did this time. I lied and told him Army Man wants to beat me up because I asked his daughter out on a date. Army Man's daughter was in my grade and beautiful. Frank goes to the front lawn ready for war. Frank is on the lawn doing karate moves. It was like something out of a Bruce Lee movie. I was upstairs looking out my window, laughing. Frank has a brown belt in karate and has high intensity. Army Man didn't want any part of Frank Kung Foo and left. After that night I was always looking over my back. He never caught me; it drove him mad. Army Man wouldn't let his daughter go anywhere near me.

In the spring of 1982, my freshman year, I played number five on Norman High's tennis team. I don't think I ever lost in singles. At three doubles my partner JG and I won a lot. Our tennis coach was a football coach. Our top six in order was PK, MF, KW, KC, EM, and JG. I played at five singles all season and three doubles. The regular season was over and it's a week before state.

The number seven on Norman High's tennis team wanted to challenge me. Whoever won was in the top six and went to State. The coach told me that since I was a freshman, I would have plenty of time to play at State in the future. He is going to let this senior challenge me. I told him, why doesn't he challenge the number six for State. My coach told me the number six is a senior and deserves to go to State. By now I'm cussing the coach out with furious anger. I have a meltdown and was cussing the whole team out. We play the challenge match in front of everyone I just cussed out. The whole team is rooting for the senior. I'm playing so mad that I can't focus. I lost, now I'm not going to State. I quit Norman High's tennis team for life right then and there.

In 1982 Mary's evil dad died and good riddance. My parents go to Toledo, Ohio to the funeral for a week. Craig and Jennifer have a party while their gone. People parked in the front lawn and all over Poplar Lane. I'm at the party with my friend BT. One of Jennifer's friends starts a fight with one of Craig's friends. While fighting they broke our tv and stereo. I told Craig and Jennifer I'm leaving and whatever happens is on them.

I spend the night with my friend BT. The next morning BT and I drive to Poplar Lane. I turn the corner and can't see our house. Our house is the only two-story house on Poplar Lane. Our house was burned halfway to the ground. I see my cat, Orange Crush, dead in the front yard. I'm having a massive panic attack. I go searching through the rubble to see if there are any dead bodies. Thank God there were no bodies to be found. Everybody left the party before the fire was out of control. I go to Susan's apartment to tell her what happened. We call our parents in Ohio and they came home early. We found out wear Craig and Jennifer were hiding out. The fire started from one of Jennifer's friends. She was putting plastic Wonder Bread wrapping in the toaster and watching it flame up. When the fire department came it was too late.

Our fire insurance paid for our house to be rebuilt; it took six months. The insurance company told us to make a list of what we lost in the fire. We all lied and said we lost way more than we did. We all got a big money check and went on a shopping spree. We were glad our house burned. The insurance paid to replace my only Red Head tennis racquet for two brand new Wilson Graphite Ultra tennis racquets. That was the biggest upgrade in tennis racquet history. In 1982 on April 16th, I turned sixteen years old. At West Mid High I was driving our 1972 Buick station wagon. I could jam ten of my friends in the station wagon. My friends are NS the actor, JH the Cali surfer, B. Stalcup (AKA Mutant Beast), BT, Scraggs, Cocky, Busey, RC, JD, WE, MJ, Ruby, RM, DH, DS, LM, JB, and more. On weekends, my friend Cocky could get beer from his work. Cocky always had a bag of weed on him. Back then if you got pulled over by the Norman police they would pour out all our beer and let us go.

Chapter Seven

*1983 Frank and Mary's Marriage /
Craig's Relaxing Vacation to New Orleans*

*Even though I walk through the valley of the shadow of death, I
will fear no evil, for you are with me, your rod and your staff, they
comfort me.*

—Psalm 23:4

–Nervous Breakdown, Black Flag

In 1983 my parents' marriage was doomed. Frank cheated on Mary
years earlier. That's why they were fighting all the time. I knew
Frank and Mary were getting a divorce before anyone. Susan already moved out by then. Craig and Jennifer where on the opposite
side of the top floor. One day in 1983, I stayed home from school
sick. Everyone is gone except Mary; she didn't know I was home.
Mary called some guy she works with to come over. This little
dude had long hair, a greasy mustache, and a cowboy hat. They
were in Frank and Mary's room having sex really loud. I had
thoughts of going on the attack. I didn't do it and kept quiet. When
Frank came home from work I told him what happened. Frank and
Mary had the worst fight of all time. That night Mary told me that
all this crap was my fault. I knew it wasn't my fault, but I stayed
mad at my mom anyways. My mom and Cowboy both worked at

Children's hospital; so does Frank. You can see that's a huge problem. Frank wanted to snap Cowboy's neck. I knew Frank Kung Foo would do it. I was worried he would go to jail and get fired. I went to work with Frank the next day. I was going to fight Cowboy in his place. At Children's Hospital I told Frank I was going to get some candy. I went down to where Mary and Cowboy worked. I walked right by my mom and went right up to Cowboy. In front of thirty of my mom's coworkers I told Cowboy I was going to kill him. Before I had the chance to wrestle Cowboy, Frank stopped me. Frank took me upstairs to his office and calmed me down. After Frank saw what I almost did he left Cowboy alone. That whole incident gave me furious anger and depression. What's crazy is my mom and dad didn't get divorced for a long time. They stayed in their room and fought. It was getting old.

In tenth grade at West Mid High Frank had a light blue 1964 Lincoln Continental with suicide doors. A friend of my dad let him borrow the 64 Lincoln because I totaled the station wagon. I can't believe he let me drive the Hot Rod Lincoln. Now I'm drinking and getting high into oblivion. I'm going into oblivion with my friend Cocky. Cocky and I weren't normal beer drinking teenagers. One night Craig Miller taught us how to shotgun beer. Our goal was to shotgun a beer in three seconds or less. Cocky and I were raising hell in Norman in the Hot Rod Lincoln.

In 1983 there was another funeral. My mom's codependent mother died. Right after her evil drunken husband died. Mary and my bro Craig went to Ohio for the funeral. My mom's brother Carey, the one who was beaten into bloody sheets? Well, about eleven years earlier Uncle Carey committed robbery at a bank. Carey had a big family and went to prison. Back to the funeral. Carey asked my mom for her inheritance; ten thousand dollars. He scammed my mom and said the money was for a legitimate business. Mary gave Carey the money. She came back to Norman, Oklahoma in her mother's car. Carey asked Craig if he wanted to go back to New Orleans, Louisiana. Uncle Carey's legitimate business was running a whore house and dealing drugs.

Carey's Brothel was right down the street from Bourbon Street. Craig loved it. Craig had all the drugs on the planet at his disposal. Carey gave Craig a job driving ladies to their destination as their bodyguard. Imagine a twenty-or-more-year-old, long-haired, hippy tennis player driving prostitutes around New Orleans. Craig was there too long and didn't want to come back. My parents made Craig come home. Craig loaded up some of our grandma's furniture in a Ryder truck.

Before Craig left New Orleans, Uncle Carey gave Craig a bunch of weed. Carey also gave him a joint laced with PCP. Craig smoked the joint right before he hit the road. PCP makes you hallucinate way too hard. You don't know what's real or not; it's a nightmare. Craig is hallucinating and paranoid driving back to Oklahoma. Craig thinks the FBI is following him all through Louisiana. Craig makes it to Texas and is freaking out. He pulls over on the highway and runs for it. Craig is wearing tennis shorts and tennis shoes. Craig ran through the deep brush and thorns like Tarzan. All the sudden he's in a small Texas town. He ran up to some people on their porch. Craig asked them to hide him. Of course, they told him to go away. He ran to a funeral parlor and asked the director to hide him. The director told him to get out of here, or he's calling the police. Craig ran back to the Ryder truck. No one was ever following him and he hallucinated the whole thing.

Still freaking out, Craig drove nonstop to Children's Hospital in OKC. Craig still thinks the FBI is following him. Craig turns himself in to security at Children's Hospital. Craig could have gotten away with his weed, but PCP wouldn't let him. The cops go to my dad's office at work. They tell Frank that his son is in jail for possession of a bunch of weed. Frank bails him out of jail; now Craig is facing prison time. While Craig is waiting for his trial he lost his mind. He thought he was going to prison. He started training

8
CRAIG MILLER
1983

to survive prison. Craig was lifting, running, and picking fights. Craig kept telling me he was the baddest man alive. He wasn't bad at all; he was just scared to death. Craig Miller is the nicest guy ever. For the first time in my life, he scared me.

One day before his trial, Craig and I went to OU Varsity tennis courts to play a two-out-of-three set match. I've never come close to beating my brother in my life. Craig is five years older than me with a cannon serve. OU men's tennis team were practicing next to us. On the other side were a court of ladies playing doubles. Craig is killing me like always. The only way I have a chance of beating Craig is to call everything out and cuss him out. Craig is so mad he can't focus or play. I won the second set. We are cussing each other out at the top of our lungs. Some OU tennis players told us to be quiet. I had to stop Craig from attacking the OU men's tennis team. Craig was turning into a werewolf and fangs were coming out. The ladies playing next to us quit playing and left.

We were in the third set, five all, and the OU team is watching our insane match. All the sudden Craig quietly tells me to come to the net. I'm cussing him out while walking to the net. Craig lets out a war call from hell and punches me in the chest. I ran home angry and my back was killing me. I had whiplash from the punch it was so hard. My dad took me to the Norman Emergency Room. My friend LM that I ran cross country with, her dad was the ER doctor in Norman for a long time.

The ER doctor asked me how it happened. I told him the truth. The doctor was mad at Craig. My back was so bad I could barely move or walk. The ER doctor gave me a prescription for opioid painkillers. Right when I came home, Craig pushed me down on the ground. He took my painkillers and ran off.

A couple weeks later Craig and I got into it again. This time he kicked me in the ribs a few times. I went back to LM's dad at the ER. This time he was pissed off. He said, I know it's your brother, but I'm calling the police. I lied and told him, I got into a fight with a big dude on campus.

Right before Craig's trial we had a small party on Poplar Lane. Craig had some friends over and I had Cocky and WE over. Craig was hammered drunk and picking fights with his friends. I came up with a plan to get him back for the ER visits from running through my neighborhood constantly. I knew where a wicked cactus patch was at the end of the street.

It was nighttime. I go in the party and punch Craig in the arm. He turned into a drunk werewolf and chases me down the street. Craig is right behind me. I'm running the fastest two-hundred-yard dash of my life. I jump over the cactus and Craig doesn't. Craig rips through the long cactus patch. My plan to take Craig out worked perfectly. I'm laughing at Craig and he's on the ground crying. Craig is asking for help, and I walk back to the party. I take him to his room upstairs. He asked me to get his bible for him. He is sitting up full of cactus needles and crying. That morning Frank comes home to a bunch of passed out dudes. There's a pair of Puma shoes and a Bjorn Borg Donnay wood tennis racquet in the front lawn. The Borg Donnay racquet was warped from the rain that night. That made me mad because I loved that racquet. Frank and I check on Craig; he's still sitting up full of needles. He puked on his bible and he's still crying. A while later Craig finally went to his trial. The judge's verdict for all that weed was just probation. Thank God Craig instantly turned back into his old, nice self. To this very day, I bring up the cactus patch story constantly. Craig and I have a good laugh.

In the spring of 1983, I got over my anger toward Norman High's tennis coach. I didn't quit, I worked too hard not to play. In 1983 in the Oklahoma High School State Tennis Tournament, my buddy MF did well at number one singles. MF might have won number one singles, I can't remember. I was in the semifinals of number two singles. I was beating the number one seed. I won the first set and was up in the second set. We were the only match left for the day. Everybody came over to watch us play. When people watch me play my anxiety gets bad. I couldn't play anymore and was having a massive anxiety attack. The dude came back and won the second set. He also won the third set easy. Now I'm playing for third place. I killed the guy because no one was watching. I got third place at number two singles at State. I might have peeked in tennis in 1983 my sophomore year.

Chapter Eight

1984 Frank and Mary's Divorce / The Drugstore Bandit

Be not overly wicked, neither be a fool. Why should you die before your time?

—Ecclesiastes 7:17

–Mad World, Tears for Fears

1984 was an extremely dark year. My mom and dad finally got divorced. The only good thing about 1984 was a girl. Her nickname is Ambee. One night I was driving Franks red Porsche 924 around Norman. I went to a party that night. I said, do any of you girls want to go driving around in my Porsche. Ambee threw a girl out of the way and jumped in the Porsche. After that night we dated for the next two years. It was my first love and made life bearable. If another girl looked at me Ambee was ready to fight her. I love Ambee's parents; they took me in as one of the family.

My depression from my parents' divorce attacked me like a looter in a riot. In 1984, after the divorce, Frank, Jennifer, Craig, and I were still living on Poplar Lane. At the time Susan met a Cool Dude. Cool Dude was a Petroleum Engineer graduate from the University of Oklahoma. Mary was living by herself in OKC on Lincoln Blvd. Frank was dating my future stepmom and they married in record time. After the wedding we all moved to Brookhaven on Brookview Street in Norman.

Our new family fusion is Frank, Craig, Jennifer, and I. Fused with my stepmom, stepsister, and stepbrother Chili Pepper. Jennifer moved in with her older boyfriend in a house on Flood Street. Living in Brookhaven there were a lot of strict rules. Before living with my stepmom, I was never grounded in my life. I stayed in my room for a whole semester at Norman High. I had no idea what to do, my mind was bending. What's funny is my stepbrother Chili Pepper and my relationship was like the movie *Stepbrothers*. At first, we thought we were too cool to hang out with each other. Chili Pepper was a skateboarding punk rocker. And I was a cocky tennis player. We had two things in common. Our love for the B-52's and partying hard.

I quit running and playing tennis. I was top four on the cross-country team and two on the tennis team. During that year people were wondering what happened to me. My cross-country and tennis coach were trying to get ahold of me. My dad had no clue what to do with me. After I laid in my room for a semester I asked God for help. God told me to get out of the house and run. I went for a long jog and was back in life.

I went back to Norman High in the spring of '84. I was ineligible to play tennis for Norman High. Not playing tennis for a year killed my game. Everybody got better and I went backward. I might as well quit playing tennis for five years, that's how bad I was. I turned my depression into anger. I was my old self again but angry as hell. I started raising hell at the house in Brookhaven. My stepmom grounded me constantly. I would break curfew coming home late. My stepmom had a little Yorkshire Terrier named Mitsy. Mitsy would bust me every time trying to sneak in my window at three in the morning.

In 1984 Craig was going to Central State University in Edmond, Oklahoma. He tried to walk on the men's tennis team. The coach didn't want him around because of his drug reputation. Craig could have played high up for CSU. Craig just went to school and partied. I don't blame CSUs coach for not letting Craig play because Craig was living in an apartment across the street from campus. Craig's roommate is the Drugstore Bandit.

Drugstore Bandit was going around Edmond robbing pharmacies. He was breaking in through the roof of pharmacies at night. Drugstore Bandit was taking all the good drugs he could take. Drugstore Bandit was cooking down the pills into liquid form. Then shooting them into his arm intravenously with a needle. Drugstore Bandit had massive motivation to keep robbing pharmacies. I started going to Edmond to buy pills from Drugstore Bandit. After a couple more pharmacy robberies, Drugstore Bandit sold pills to a dude. This dude was caught with the pills on him by the police. Dude came over one night with a wire on. The Edmond police took Drugstore Bandit down. Drugstore Bandit went to prison for a while. Thank God Craig didn't get in trouble for being Drugstore Bandit's roommate. Think about how all this real-life action sounds insane. To the Miller family it was becoming normal.

Chapter Nine

1985 Angry Young Man / Steppenwolf and The Guess Who

Refrain from anger, and forsake wrath! Fret not yourself, it tends only to evil.

—Psalm 37:8

–People Are People, Depeche Mode

In 1985 I was a senior at Norman High School. My tennis was making a comeback. I was still dating Ambee and my grades were in serious trouble. I had to take extra classes to get eligible to play tennis. Susan and Cool Dude are still going strong. Jennifer moved out of the flood house back to Brookview. My stepmom, stepsister, Frank, Jennifer, and I are living on Brookview.

My friends at the time are, NS the actor, JH the Cali Surfer, Cocky, the Twins, Jaxon, Ambee, MJ, Ruby, B. Stalcup (AKA Mutant Beast), Scraggs, Busey, and Jennifer Miller. One of the best tennis players in Norman High's history is MF. MF is number one on Norman High's tennis team. Just for the record, MF is not a "M.F." I have to admit the initials to his name are funny. I was playing good tennis and beating some good number two players. Oklahoma high school tennis is no joke. In California I wouldn't start for a bunch of high school tennis teams. My only goal was to get a scholarship to play college tennis. I started to play about four to five hours of tennis every day. MF already had a scholarship to play tennis at OU.

One day on Brookview I started a shower. I went to my room to get my towel. Before I could get back to my shower. My stepmom stopped the shower and yelled at me for wasting water. I called her the worst possible name ever. She yelled for Frank to come and chill me out. I'm down the hallway calling my dad a wussy. Frank ran at me full speed ready for war. I took him down and put him in a headlock. My stepmom called the cops. I got in my Toyota Tercel and went to the Twins' house. The Twins were a grade lower than me. They were friends with my girlfriend Ambee. The Twins are two beautiful, sweet girls that loved to party. Their mom always let me move in when I ran from the cops. I'm living with them and going to Norman High. My dad had no idea where I went. I called Frank up and he just wanted me home. So, I went back.

Another day after school on Brookview, I made a delicious double cheeseburger with crispy bacon; it was a masterpiece. I went to the bathroom and before I got back my stepsister threw my cheeseburger in the trash. She told me that I broke one of the house rules and that she was going to tell her mom. I told her I was going to kill her. Then I chased her down the hallway. I wasn't homicidal and wasn't going to touch her. I just liked to tell people that I wanted to kill them. She locked herself in her room, then called her mom at work. They called the cops and I moved in with the Twins again.

My stepmom wanted the cops to take me to jail bad. One Saturday morning at eight AM, I heard the doorbell ring. My step-mom comes in my room gleaming with joy. She told me that I have a visitor. I go to the door in my underwear. There are two Norman police officers at the door. They told me I didn't pay a speeding ticket. They have a warrant for my arrest. I begged them to let me put on some clothes. I didn't want to go to jail in my underwear.

They followed me to my room, and I put on some clothes. They hand cuffed me and took me to Norman jail. I've never seen a bigger smile in my life on my stepmoms face that day.

In 1985, during my senior year, we had a new tennis coach for Norman High. Our new coach FB is a Norman legend and a good tennis player. One day at tennis practice at Norman High's courts, our coach was announcing everybody's grade point average, and eligibility for spring tennis. The girls and guys teams were sitting on the bleachers. Coach starts announcing all these players great grade point averages. I'm next and he tells everyone that I have a grade point average of 2.4. Half the team are laughing and I'm about to blow. Coach probably should have done that in private. I'm insecure about my learning disability. My most memorable tennis moments at Norman High in 1985. One day at tennis practice, a guy on my team and I were arguing. The poor guy called me the R word. I snapped and picked him up, upside down. I put him headfirst in a big trash can. Right in front of the girls and guys tennis team. The R word for me was like calling a Black dude the N word. It's not cool bra!

Another day at Norman High's tennis courts, Norman High was playing Casady High in a dual match. MF and I were playing their number one doubles team. One of Casady's players is the best high school tennis player I've ever seen. He was returning serves back so fast and accurate. He was nailing me in my chest before I could get ready to volley. My volleys were terrible anyways. This dude kept hitting me in my chest and laughing. I threatened to attack him if he didn't stop. He stopped and apologized. Everything was cool except the score of our match. Later in life, this dude from Casady High. He went on to play the number one in the world in a major tournament and won a set of him. The dude from Casady was ranked high in the world at the time.

One night I went cruising around drunk on tequila. I was with my buddy NS the actor. I saw a guy with the fastest car in Norman. I chased him down and asked him to race. I was in my Toyota Tercel, and he made fun of it. I got out of my car and ran at him. He blasted me with nunchucks in my forehead. I was bleeding so much that it looked like something in a horror movie. I still wanted to fight, then he threatened me with his gun. For my friend's sake I got the heck out of there. I went home to my step-mom and dad freaking out. Frank wraps my head up like the Mummy. I went to school on Monday with a swollen forehead. I was wearing sunglasses to hide my black eyes. I went to tennis practice and fainted on the court with a concussion.

I went to the ER, and they stitched my forehead up. The doctor gave me opioid painkillers. My stepmom wouldn't let me have them. She flushed them down the toilet. I went crazy and my stepmom called the cops. I moved back in with the Twins again. The Twins were my second family my senior year. I should have moved in with the Twins for good. Frank made me go to a psy-chologist for all my problems.

One night I went to Steppenwolf and The Guess Who at the Civic Center. I went with The Twins, Jaxon, and some other girls. That night one of the Twins and I took LSD. I took two hits, and she took one. It was her first-time taking LSD. She was having a bad trip. I spent most of the concert trying to calm her down. She finally went with it and had a good time. After the concert we all went back to the Twin's house. I broke curfew again and had to go home. I'm on LSD walking home in the woods. I started hearing scary noises like someone was chasing me. Then I heard a voice say, "Eric, this is Satan, I'm going to take your soul."

I yelled, "You have to catch me first." I ran through the woods like a cat. All the sudden I'm at my house on Brookview. My dad asked me why I was late. I told him that Satan is trying to take my soul. I don't have time to be grounded.

1985 the Oklahoma High School State Tennis Tournament

OU and OSUs coaches were watching my first round at two singles. I don't know why they were watching my match. I was hoping they would go away. I had another panic attack and lost first round bad. I played all season for that performance at State. Now everybody graduated from Norman High, class of 1985. I had to take one more class in the summer to graduate.

I played more tennis that summer than I ever had in my life. I went into nuclear tennis war mode. I would hit on the ball machine forever. Then I would find the best player I could and play that person until I dropped. I started playing on a level I never thought was possible. I was playing good tennis again. I was playing a lot of men's open tennis tournaments that summer.

At the end of the summer, in a tournament, I ran full sprint to a ball and something in my groin area ripped. I went to the doctor, he told me it's not a groin tear. It's something else and I need to see a Urologist. I found out I have epididymitis. It's an injury in my testicles. I could hardly walk; my tennis days were over. I was getting depressed as hell again.

I took a year of college and lived with Frank and my stepmom. All I did was work on my nut recovery. My older sister Susan and Cool Dude got married. They had their wedding reception in Norman at a big clubhouse. The night before the reception I went to a party. I took a bunch of Valium and drank a lot of beer.

I left the party and drove fast down main street. I passed out cold at the wheel. My car went to the right and crushed a curb. I hit someone's front steps at their house. I backed my car into the street in front of the house. I threw my keys over a fence and tried to walk home. I fell in the middle of the street. Then a couple cop cars surrounded me. They woke me up and asked me some questions. I told the police I was walking home from a party. They put me in Norman jail in the drunk tank. I should have gotten a DUI.

My keys were nowhere to be found. Back then you could get away with a lot more than today. All I got was a public drunk.

I got out of jail just in time to go to Susan and Cool Dudes wedding reception. All I wanted out of life at this point was to play college tennis in the fall of '86. I was playing as much as my injury would allow. I was playing in the Norman Open men's singles in the summer of '86. The coach from East Central University in Ada, Oklahoma was watching me play my first-round match with my dad. After the match they both came up to me. The coach gave me a full ride to play for ECU. I told the coach that I have an older brother that can beat me bad. He gave Craig and I full rides. Finally, I achieved my life's goal playing college tennis. At this point, I had been to jail twice, had gotten beaten up bad, had gotten an epididymitis injury, and Ambee had dumped me. My senior year was so hard on me that it broke me and humbled me. I let my anger go and made peace with my stepmom and stepsister. I now get along great with them; I love you ladies.

Chapter Ten

1986 College Tennis Ada, Oklahoma / The Big Weed Bust

Oh, taste and see that the lord is good, blessed is the man who trusts in him.

—Psalm 34:8

–The Whole Electric Album, The Cult
–The Whole Straight Outta Compton Album, NWA

To get in East Central University in Ada, Oklahoma I first had to take the ACT. I made a seven on it my first try. Then I made a great score of nine my second try. At this point I'm definitely not playing college tennis ever. I have a friend I play tennis with a lot, Juicy Little Chief, an American Indian. We are the same height, weight, and we both have brown-hair. Juicy was going to OU at the time. I begged Juicy to take my ID and take the ACT for me. I told him to give them my name and my ID only. If the ACT people thought something was wrong, Juicy's plan was to rip my ID from their hand and run like a madman. Juicy told me he would do it for INXS concert tickets at the Zoo Amphitheater. Juicy made a nineteen on it and he tried to do bad. My desperate attempt to play college tennis worked. A couple weeks later Juicy and I went to INXS front row. I paid for the tickets and Juicy's mushrooms.

Craig and I showed up to ECUs campus ready for tennis

and the ladies. The year before, ECU was dead last in the OIC Conference. ECUs new tennis team was Craig Miller and I. We knew this guy that played tennis for Ada High, AL. We talked him into playing with us. Then we saw a dude hitting next to us at practice, DP. He was good and we talked him into playing. I tried to talk Juicy Little Chief into playing for ECU. Juicy didn't do it and he would have started for ECU. That fall there was a dude on ECUs tennis team, JT. He was from Tulsa, and he was close to Craig's level. At Christmas break, JT went back to Tulsa. I wish he would have stayed. JT and Craig could have gone to nationals at one doubles.

Our tennis coach, HW, was the coolest man in the world. He was about seventy-three years old and a legend in Ada. As long as we were winning, he didn't care what we did. Craig and I are going to classes trying to look cool. Craig's brilliant and I'm taking the easiest classes possible. Our tennis coach let us move into one of his houses a block from campus. It quickly turned into a college party house. One day at tennis practice, I noticed a bunch of girls driving by. I had a brilliant idea. I told Craig to play with his shirt off. All the sudden carloads of girls were stopping to watch us practice. I would go up to the car and make moves. It was insane how easy it was to meet girls with Craig as my bait.

In spring of 1987, ECU played all the OIC Conference tennis teams. I think we beat them all. The day we played Oklahoma City University in OKC. They were one of the best teams in NAIA tennis. Aussie OKC from the tennis boom is their head coach. That day OCU played their number six at one. I have no idea what they were doing. I think it was to prove their worst player could smoke our best. OCUs whole tennis team were cocky Aussies except the number six. I had to play their number one that day. Craig is killing their number six on the next court. I'm getting sand blasted by their number one. I heard the Aussie I was playing was a heavyweight golden gloves boxer. I get a game off Golden Gloves. On that game change he elbows me in my chest. I start cussing him out then he gets in my face. My brother Craig comes over to my court. He tells Golden Gloves to come on with it. Golden Gloves looked at Craig very carefully. Golden Gloves didn't want to fight Craig Miller that day. If they would have fought that day at OCU the fight would have been against a good Australian boxer vs a mutant American wrestler. That would have been the tennis fight of the century. Craig beat the number six for OCU, six zero six zero. OCUs number six has the same first name as my brother. Today CG from Ardmore is a famous preacher in OKC. By the way, Australian tennis players are the cockiest in the world.

During that time Craig needed a weight room with more weights. Craig asked our coach to talk to ECUs football coach. Coach told Craig to come lift in the football weight room. That day ECUs football team just finished lifting. They were wondering why we were in there. Craig goes up to a football player. He asked him if he was finished bench pressing two hundred pounds. The whole football team was watching Craig about to lift two hundred pounds. They were making fun of the tennis wussy. Warming up, Craig did more reps than the football player before him. The head football coach asked Craig to try out for the football team. Craig turned it down; he can't get injured for tennis. That was one of the coolest things I've ever witnessed.

At the time my mom Mary stopped drinking. She was heavily into Alcoholics Anonymous. She lived in Oklahoma City and married a dude from AA. Mary's new husband is a crack head and cheating on her. One day Mary was at her apartment while her husband was gone. A friend of my mom's husband knocked on her door. Mary knew the guy and opened her door. That bastard put a gun to my mom's head and raped her. When my mom told Craig and I what happened, we begged Mary to tell us what apartment the rapist lived in. We were going to beat him close to death. He probably would have put our head out with a bullet. Mary knew better; she didn't want us to die. She didn't report it to the police. She was scared this guy was going to come back and kill her. All Mary did was move to a safer part of OKC, with her greasy husband. This is sad. A lot of women that are raped do not report it. Because of humiliation and retaliation.

In the spring of 1987, the OIC Conference tennis tournament was in Durant, Oklahoma at Southeastern's tennis courts. First round in two singles my nut injury was killing me. I had to default my match. That took away points for the tournament. During the finals of number one singles, Craig was being harassed. The whole Southeastern football team started watching Craig's match because their dorm was next to the courts. They did everything they could to mess with my brother, calling him Bjorn Borg wussy and threating to kick his butt. Still, with all the pressure, Craig won number one singles easy. In the finals of three doubles, my partner DP and I were playing Southwestern. The match went to the third set; it was a war. We were playing on center court and everybody was watching. Southeastern football players were still harassing us. Imagine playing the most important match of your life with football players threating you. I took a Valium before the match to be calm. We won the third set, and the match. ECU were co-champions in the OIC Conference. I felt bad for defaulting my singles match. We might have won it clean. The 1987 ECU OIC Conference Co-Champs in order: Craig Miller, Eric Miller, AL, WH, DA, and DP. Our coach HW received coach of the year in the OIC Conference. He was so happy, and he deserved it.

In the fall of 1987, a new batch of good players showed up at ECU. We beat some good teams that fall. That was the best ECU team I played on. The fall of 1987 ECUs men's tennis team were Craig Miller, Eric Miller, BM, DR, JN, and SS. At the end of that fall, I injured my epididymis again. I couldn't play in the spring of '88.

The County Fair Comes to Ada

Craig Miller entered the tough man competition at heavyweight. Craig had to fight a big Black dude first round. This dude was big and could fight. In the fight, Craig picked the dude up and threw him. In a tough man fight you can only box. Wresting is against the rules. Craig lost and looked like he was run over by a train. Craig had two black eyes, a messed-up nose, and a blown ankle. Craig Miller is a madman.

In the spring of 1988, Craig had another great year at number one. ECU men's tennis did really well at the OIC Conference tournament. After not playing that spring, I went into a massive depression. I found a dude that sold me painkillers and Xanax. I started taking those pills quiet often. Craig's eligibility was over and he got a job for the Ada Highway Department. Craig was on the sign crew and fixed signs. During my injury I was talking to God again. I was asking God for healing power. It's amazing how easy it is, to ask God for something when you're hurting. When you're feeling great you blow God off. What I just said pertains to me.

One weekend I went to Juicy Little Chief's house in Norman. We watched an OU basketball game. We drank hard and fast like always. When my friends passed out, I decided to go for a ride. It was at two in the morning in Norman and I was blind drunk. Nothing was going on, but I finally found some action. The OU police were chasing me around campus. My music was full blast, and my car didn't have a rear-view mirror. The OU police had to get right next to me, to know they were there. I pulled into an OU dorm acting like I lived there. I started jogging to the dorm hoping they would go away. The OU police tackled me and were furious. The OU police took me to the Norman jail. I got my first DUI. Right before the spring of 1989, I was sitting in my living room in Ada and the doorbell rings. It's Jennifer Miller and her boyfriend

Craig Miller

Eric Miller

from California. They drove all the way from Cali wanting to move in. I let them move in and her boyfriend made me nervous. Jennifer enrolls at ECU and goes out for the women's tennis team. Jennifer hasn't played tennis since she was eleven years old. In the spring of '89 Jennifer made the number six spot for the girl's team. Jennifer is chain smoking cigarettes, weed, and doing methamphetamines. She's doing all these drugs while playing for a college tennis team. There was meth everywhere in Ada, Oklahoma.

In the spring of 1989, I was number one on East Central's tennis team. BM from Ardmore was my doubles partner. We were an average number one doubles team and played great together.

I was on opioid painkillers and Xanax. On those pills I played great. Xanax took away my nerves and painkillers killed my pain. On those pills I didn't think, I let muscle memory take over. In the spring of '89, the OIC Conference Tennis Tournament was in Alva, Oklahoma at Northwestern University's courts. The night before the conference tournament in our hotel I talked half the team into going out that night. I stole my coach's keys to the team van. Now, I'm driving ECUs tennis team to a bar in Alva. In a big Van with ECU sports plastered on the side of it. We got back to the hotel at two in the morning. The room I was staying in with my doubles partner; he kicked me out of the room. He had a girl in there from the bar. I bought a twelve pack of beer and got hammered drunk in the ECU van all night

Around seven AM everybody's getting ready for their matches. I'm seeing double and about to puke. HW is yelling at me in the parking lot at the hotel, telling me that if I don't do really well at number one today, he's taking my scholarship away; he was furious. First round in number one singles, I had to play the number one for Northwestern from Alva. He was a cool dude from Sweden. We had a three-set war; I was puking through the fence. My coach was watching me big time. He kept saying, "You better not lose you little SOB." He called me a little SOB a lot. I finally win the third set. I made it to the semifinals against one of the best players in the nation. This cool Black dude TT played one for Northeastern.

TT and I played together on Norman High's tennis team. He was a couple years younger than me. Since we were friends, I asked him for a favor. I asked him, no matter how bad you beat me, please say the score was close and he said no problem. Before the match we had a lunch break. The Swede asked me if I wanted to go to his dorm room and party. The Swede had an ice chest full of beer and weed. We pounded beer and got higher than a madman while the rest of the team went to eat food like normal people. I was ready for the semis against my friend. I was way too high; it felt like a weird dream. TTbeat me bad and turned in the fake score. He said the score was close. It worked, because no one watched our match. My coach was so happy with my fake score. He gave me a full ride for the next year. In the finals of number one singles, TT beat a really good player from Southwestern six zero, six zero.

After the spring of 1989, Craig let a guy move into our house that was selling weed. He sold it to college and high school students. I was telling Craig to kick him out. Craig and Jennifer loved smoking weed so much. They kept telling me to shut up and he's staying. I started noticing Ada police circling our house constantly. The Ada police were watching us bigtime. I moved into another one of my coaches' houses. Two weeks later, I got a phone call from a friend. She told me to watch the ten o'clock news. The dude, Craig, and Jennifer were busted by the Ada police. The big weed bust was live on the Ada tv station. The tv anchorman was in our front yard talking about the bust. Dude, Craig, Jennifer, and a couple more people were being taken to jail.

I called my attorney from my DUI. He came down to Ada and bailed Craig and Jennifer out. That next week, I was told to get out of Ada a few times. We had to leave town; college tennis was over. Life went from a beautiful dream to a nightmare overnight. Depression is kicking in once again. I am so sick and tired of being down. Craig and Jennifer were facing jail time. In the trial they both got probation. After the weed bust we moved back to Norman, Oklahoma. Craig, Jennifer, and I moved into an apartment together. We had no clue what we were going to do next.

Chapter Eleven

1990 Depeche Mode Violator Tour /
College Tennis Head Coach / Craig Visits the Nut House

A heart that devises wicked plans, feet that run rapidly to evil.

—Proverbs 6:18

–400 Bucks, Reverend Horton Heat

I started using Xanax and opioid pain killers playing college tennis.
I loved the high and Jennifer could get all those pills anytime. All
I wanted out of life, was to make just enough money to party for a
living. Craig got a job at Club Santa in OKC as the maintenance
man. One of the owners and the director of tennis is Aussie OKC.
Aussie OKC is from the tennis boom shalock lock boom!

There were a lot of cocky Aussie tennis pros working
there. Craig got me a job at Club Santa making sandwiches in the
deli. I got Juicy Little Chief a job there working the front desk.
Club Santa had a big men's open tennis tournament. No one knew
Craig could play tennis. Craig beat Aussie OKC in his own tournament. Aussie OKC walked off the court mad. He yelled, "I just
lost to my fricking maintenance man." Craig was one of the best
maintenance men in tennis in the country.

1990 Depeche Mode Comes to Dallas, Texas

At the Starplex on their Violator tour, four American Indian friends and I pack into a little car. We drove from Norman, Oklahoma to the concert. We get a cheap hotel room in Denton, Texas. When we got to the show the band Nitzer Ebb opened for D Mode. Nitzer Ebb has an electronic, hard, fast-cracking beat. I've never heard of Nitzer Ebb before the concert. Nitzer Ebb is a great band in the fast-cracking beat category. D Mode is my favorite band of all time. And that's a bold statement coming from me. After the concert three of my friends went back to the hotel. My big American Indian friend KD and I took a taxi to the Video Bar in Dallas.

We were at the Video Bar for an hour. D Mode literally walk in the bar. I went up to them and asked every dude in D Mode, "Why are some of your songs blasphemous to God?" Then I asked them, "What do you think God is going to say to you when you try to get into heaven?" Yes, that is the first thing I said to my favorite band. DG, the lead singer's reply to my question was to F off. AF, the keyboard player's reply to my question was, "I want a drink." I couldn't ask AW the question; he wanted privacy with his girlfriend. MG, the best song writer of all time, laughed at my question. I explained to MG that my question was a joke. MG and I started to hang out at the bar. He kept buying me beers and shots all night because I was broke. My friend KD was partying hard with DG and AF. D Mode back then partied harder than I did. When the Video Bar was about to close MG invited KD and I to a small party in the Video Bar all night. I couldn't stay, I was way too drunk. I asked KD to get me back to the hotel. Thank you, MG for one of the coolest nights of my life.

This Story is for My Stepbrother, Chili Pepper

During this time, Chili Pepper and I go to the Oktoberfest downtown OKC. We were chugging tons of beer and a wild Black dude comes up to us. This dude told us his name was The Governor. The Governor asked us if we wanted to smoke crack. The Governor took us to a crack house across the street. The house had like six Black dudes hanging out and one old Black lady running the show. We walk in and the house had the old school rap band UTFO playing. It was a trip! Chili Pepper bought about forty dollars in crack. The house made us share the crack with everybody. By the time the pipe came around to us. We only got a couple hits each. While we were cracking it up, a Black pimp that looked like Cool Moe D, asked us if we wanted a lady. Pimp Cool Moe D tells two ladies to come out to the living room. They were in their underwear and asked us to go in the bedroom. We said, no thank you and just smoked crack. We got tired of sharing our crack with

Me and Chilli Pepper on his 25th birthday.

everyone in the house. The Governor took us on a wild goose chase crack run. He took us all over town. We finally left The Governor at a house. We bolted back to my place, and we were freaked out. At that time in our lives. That was the craziest thing Chili Pepper and I had ever done!

In 1991 the coach at Oklahoma Christian University tennis team offered me a half ride to play for him. I was going to play anywhere from three to five on the team. Of course, my nut injury came back; I couldn't play. I became their assistant coach instead. That started my tennis teaching career. That summer a mad Aussie tennis pro friend of mine got me a job at that famous tennis academy in Bradenton, Florida. That academy also had a summer branch in Beaver Dam, Wisconsin.

A month before I went to Wisconsin, I bought a half grocery bag of magic mushrooms. My sister Jennifer could get all the drugs all the time. My wild friends and I ate all the shrooms for a month strait. These are some of my wild friends during the decadent decade of the 90s: Wild Wild Wes, Chili Pepper, Groovy Lynn, Cranky, Juicy Little Chief, Chris Wild, Cathy the Female Elvis, Greedy Creedy, Cocky, Sarah, Mad Basterd, Disco Susan G, and Jacking Jeff G. A week before I went to the academy my mind was fried chicken from shroom abuse. I kept seeing little black animals run by that weren't there. I drive my Honda to Wisconsin crying like a baby. I'm there for a month. I kept seeing things that weren't there. This is one of the scariest times of my life. I thought my mind was torched for life. While I'm teaching one day, I asked the kids. If they saw a little black dog run across the court. They looked at me funny. I acted like I was messing with them. I kept seeing a tiny black dog run by me at fifty miles per hour. At the end of the summer at the academy in Beaver Dam, I started feeling better mentally and my hallucinations were gone. Thank God that little speedy black dog never came back.

At the end of the camp my boss asked me if I wanted to

teach at the main academy in Bradenton, Florida. I did it for two weeks and one of the bosses liked my teaching. He wanted me to stay at the main academy in Bradenton, Florida for good. I declined, it was hot and hard work for low pay. In 1992 Rage Against the Machine came out with the most important rock album of all time. It tells the brutal truth about America.

In the summer of 1992, I went back to teach at the academy in Beaver Dam. This time I brought an Aussie friend of mine. My Aussie friend TL was an all-American tennis player for OCU. Another pro friend of mine was a cocky young lady from North Dakota, RV. That summer TL, RV, and I hung out a lot. In the fall I went back to OKC. I was Oklahoma Christian University's assistant coach again. I became great friends with the two best players on the team. They were from Mexico City, and they were twins.

In the fall of 1993, I got a call from HW, my old coach from ECU. He was dying from bone cancer. He wanted me to come back to Ada, Oklahoma. He wanted me to take over as head coach for ECU. He told me he wasn't going to make it to the spring. I couldn't say no to him, I loved him like a dad. I packed up all my things and moved to Ada. I'm afraid because everyone in Ada still hates me from the weed bust.

My old coach was on chemotherapy and throwing up every day. It was hard to be around him without crying. He still got mad at me and called me a little SOB. I was about to take over the most dysfunctional college tennis team in the country. The first day I was running practice and a couple of higher ups at ECU were playing tennis and one of them recognized me. He came over and said, "What in the hell are you doing here?" My old coach, HW, was friends with this dude. HW told him that I didn't have anything to do with the weed bust. The guy chilled out and everything was cool.

Right when I started coaching, two or three guys weren't coming to practice. The second-best player was nowhere to be found and became ineligible. Some of my players were arrested.

They broke into a city of Ada facility, while partying on the grounds. My players videotaped themselves partying on the grounds. When they were arrested, the Ada police had their video tape proof. On a totally other incident, one of my players was arrested for a DUI and possession of weed.

I know for a fact that God was paying me back for the way Craig and I acted, when we played for ECU. I had a couple team meetings. My rules were no drugs, come to practice and stay eligible. Only three players were following all the rules. Christmas break came and my old coach HW died. He was right; he didn't make it to the spring.

Before my old coach HW died, he knew the lady that ran the senior citizen home in Ada. He got me in there to live while coaching the team. My number one player for ECU, SL from Shawnee, lived there. SL lived in a different apartment, and we hung out a lot. We were living with hundreds of senior citizens all around us. One day my team was playing challenge matches. I wrote a short little song about big breasts called, "38s." My bands name is 427 Jet and it's just Eric Miller with a microphone. There was a karaoke bar in Ada. While the music was playing, I would sing my lyrics to "38s." One night after I sang "38s" a girl comes up to me and says she has thirty-eights and she did. She was the catcher for the ECU women's softball team. She was the biggest girl I've ever seen. She was taller and heavier than me. We went to a karaoke after party at SL apartment. Big Lady and I borrowed his bedroom. In the middle of our drunken love session the two legs break off the bottom of the bed. It was so loud it woke up ten senior citizens. They all came to the door. They asked SL what the loud noise was. The seniors thought it was a gun going off. I came out of the bedroom into the hallway. I tell the seniors the bed broke. I left out the part of me and my big lady friend.

Spring break came. ECU did not have any teams to play. My friend Big Jimmy and I went to Boca Raton, Florida to visit my brother. Craig was teaching tennis at a big-time country club in Boca. Before Craig went to Boca, he drove his old brown Honda there. Right when Craig got to Boca he pulled into a bank parking lot because his brown turd mobile caught on fire. The Boca fire department showed up, but it was too late. Craig's brown turd mobile was now a black turd mobile.

In Boca Raton Craig worked for his Aussie friend at the country club. His Aussie friend taught tennis at Club Santa in OKC, years earlier. His Aussie friend is now the director of tennis at the country club in Boca. Craig moved into an apartment by the beach. He lived with another dude that worked at the country club. Since Craig's Honda burned in the banks parking lot, Craig had to ride a bicycle seven miles one way to work. Craig was working way too many hours at the country club. Craig was working himself to death. All he did was work, drink hard, and smoke weed. After a while Craig was losing his mind from no sleep. When Big Jimmy and I showed up in Boca Raton for spring break Craig kept telling me that he was the angel of Philadelphia in the bible. Craig was freaking me out; it was scary. Craig was either crying or not talking at all. After hanging out with Craig for a week, losing his mind, I go back to Ada to coach ECU men's tennis. I call my dad Frank the child psychologist. I tell him Craig has gone mad. Frank flew to Boca Raton and put Craig on the plane. Frank and Craig came back to Norman, Oklahoma. Frank took Craig to Griffin Memorial Mental Hospital. Craig's diagnosis at the hospital was psychotic and catatonic. When I went to visit Craig, he wouldn't talk to anyone. Craig just sat there with a crazy look in his eyes. Then they sent Craig to a mental hospital in Vinita, Oklahoma.

That spring ECU men's tennis did well. I wasn't a good coach for ECU. I had the mind of a child and couldn't control the team. I went with the madness of my team instead of kicking players off. This is sad. JM from Ardmore was the player on my team that gave me the most trouble. He died of a drug overdose later in life. JM is the little brother of my doubles partner BM in 1989. The spring season was over. I had a meeting with the ECU Athletic Director (AD). The AD liked my head coaching and wanted me back another year. I quit ECU. My experience as the head coach was pure anxiety.

Chapter Twelve

1994 The Oklahoma City Tennis Business

*Therefore, be very careful how you live, not as unwise but as wise,
taking advantage of every opportunity, because the days are evil.*
—Ephesians 5:15-18

–Shamrocks and Shenanigans, House of Pain

In 1994 Susan Miller has her first child with Cool Dude. They now
have a baby boy and are living the American dream. Susan and
Cool Dude's baby boy's name is Suave C. After being the head
tennis coach at ECU I ran into a friend, RF from Shawnee. RF
taught tennis at Club OKC, in Nichols Hills. He told me they
needed another pro and I applied for the job. The director of tennis
from the Czech Republic hired me. There's no way anyone would
turn down this job. I was teaching tennis trying not to screw it up.

I was given the chance of running the junior tennis program.
I excelled; I finally found what I was best at. I started something
called pizza fun night, where parents could drop off their kids and go
do whatever they wanted. This pizza fun night was a crazy big thing.
It turned our junior program into big numbers. My plan was to get a
ton of juniors out for anything, and the pizza fun night was it.

Now, all I had to do was push the junior tennis clinics on
everyone. It worked, then I started giving the juniors a reason to

get better in tennis. We started to play junior interclub matches against other clubs. I was taking juniors to Oklahoma tennis tournaments. Within a year, Club OKC had a solid junior tennis program. My boss from the Czech Republic was extremely happy with me. Life was great and I was in love with tennis again.

While I was working at Club OKC I was going to school at the University of Central Oklahoma in Edmond, Oklahoma. UCO used to be called CSU for Central State University in Edmond. It's the same college just different names. I was trying to get a degree in sociology with a minor in chemical dependency. I wanted to become a drug and alcohol abuse counselor. I'm making passing grades in my sociology classes and loving it. One day UCO told me that I can't take anymore upper-level sociology classes. I still must take a bunch of basic courses, like college algebra, to get my associates degree first. There's no way in hell I'm passing all those classes. With my learning disability I couldn't pass basic math. That's why I made a nine on my ACT. I had to come to grips with the fact that I'm not going to become a drug and alcohol counselor. Also, how can I be a drug counselor when I'm using just as many drugs as my clients. Now I'm going all out with my tennis career. The best part of being a tennis pro was picking women up at bars. Telling them I was a tennis pro was gold.

In 1995 it was around nine AM And I had just gotten to work at Club OKC. A ladies doubles league started at nine AM. All the sudden, I heard a big boom. One of the women had to hold on to something, the ground was shaking. We were wondering what that boom was. I turned on the TV. Everybody was in shock, it was the Murrah building bombing. My dad Frank was working at Saint Anthony's Hospital at the time. I couldn't get a hold of him. I found out later he was okay. They started sending traumatized people to the hospital ER to get help with my dad for mental trauma. My dad said it was the worst day of his life.

Since my ECU tennis days, I quit playing tennis for five

years. I picked it back up with a vengeance. I started playing men's open doubles tournaments with my Aussie friends. My Aussie friends were some of the best tennis players in Oklahoma.

Now the greasy side of the OKC tennis business. Some of the teaching pros in OKC, were being sneaky greasy. Like having sex with married women that were members at their club. The husbands were attacking these pros like pissed off wolves. I couldn't understand why teaching pros wanted to die over sex. Some tennis pros had to leave OKC because of pissed off husbands threatening to kill them. I thought it was safer dating single women. I'm not judging any of those pros. I was in a circle of pros that were alcoholic drug addicts. My circle of mad tennis pros were a few Americans and a few cocky Aussies. We cared more about drugs than sex. I did anyways.

Our cocaine dealer was a madman and a good tennis player in OKC. At the time he loves and sells big exotic snakes. Every time we went to his apartment to buy cocaine his whole apartment was surrounded by big snakes in glass containers. We all used to say what if something happened. Like all his big snakes got loose and went crawling around his apartment complex. It would have been funny seeing twenty big snakes, joining the people for a swim at his apartment complex swimming pool.

My boss from the Czech Republic retired from Club OKC. The Aussie that got Craig his job at the Boca Raton country club is the soon-to-be director of tennis at Club OKC. This Aussie was telling people he was going to fire me. I was getting tired of hearing this crap. I quit and got a tennis teaching job at Club Quail in OKC. Before I quit, I got my friend Cranky a job at Club OKC. Cranky started helping with the junior tennis program. Cranky stayed at Club OKC and became a great teaching pro for them. Club Quails director of tennis is a big cocky American redneck. Redneck was a great tennis pro in playing and running Club Quail. Redneck ran the biggest and the best tennis tournaments in Oklahoma. Like his pro-am with great college players and Pros. Pros from around the country that would play with ammeters like myself. I really learned how to teach tennis working for Redneck. He was relentless about his teaching pros learning. Redneck made me take the USPTA exam in Fort Worth, Texas. The USPTA exam made me a better teaching pro than anything.

I started my pizza fun night at Club Quail, and it exploded. I wasn't the director of the junior tennis program. I brought a lot of new juniors to the club. Because of that I received employee of the month at Club Quail. Let's Rewind to 1987 when Craig and I were at ECU playing tennis. I thought Craig and I were playing great doubles together. We entered a winter men's open doubles tournament at Club Wood in OKC. I thought we were going to win this doubles tournament easy. I went up to the tour director and asked who we were playing first round. She told me they were older guys. One of them is the director of tennis at Club Quail. I yelled out we're going to kill those old dudes. Because of that everyone came to watch our match. Redneck and his partner DR beat us six zero, six one. The only reason we got one game was Craig's cannon serve. Redneck was hitting me with one hundred mile an hour shots to my body. He had me backed up to the baseline. Craig kept telling me to get my butt back to the net. It was the biggest butt kicking I've ever had in doubles. Now I'm working for Redneck. He might be cockier than any Aussie tennis pro out there.

Chapter Thirteen

1997 Frank Miller Dies / Madness in Mexico City

The Lord is near to the brokenhearted and saves the crushed in spirit.

—Psalm 34:18

You shall have no other Gods before me.

—Exodus 20:2-6

"Put Your Head Out," Manhole
This song is for women's rights. Tairrie B the rapper is my kind of woman. She doesn't take any crap from no man or no clan. You know what I'm saying.

—Eric Miller

After the nut house! Craig Miller is making his comeback. Craig has a mind-blowing moment of clarity. He gets his bachelor's degree from UCO in Edmond. Then he goes to seminary school to work full time for God. For the first time in his life, Craig is sober and mentally healthy. Jennifer Miller is starting to have drug overdoses. She was doing heroin, speed, and tons of pills. She was sharing needles with anybody. She was living dangerous.

One day I was teaching on the first court at Club Quail. I got a phone call. It's my brother-in-law Cool Dude. He tells me

Frank Miller died. I worshiped my dad like a god. He died of a massive heart attack at age sixty. He had an enlarged heart. Frank smoked cigarettes and weed for thirty years.

I took his death worse than anyone. Frank enabled me and did everything for me. Between him and using drugs, I never grew up. Frank's funeral was in Norman and there were a ton of tennis players there. Frank left me fifty thousand dollars for my inheritance. I thought I was rich.

At the time I was playing good doubles. Since I grew up in Norman, I always wanted to win the Norman open in singles or doubles. I got a six foot five South African mutant beast for my doubles partner. He was an individual national title winner in singles and doubles for UCO in Edmond. He is one of the nicest dudes I've ever met. We taught tennis together at Club Quail. I told him I would give him a hundred dollars if we win. We played the Norman open at a tennis center on the west side of Norman where they had a memorial bench in honor of my dad, Frank Miller. That day I sat on my dad's bench crying. We made it to the finals against two good ex college players. We split sets; a crowd is now watching. I popped a couple of Valium earlier for nerves. It wasn't working, I was still nervous. I had a high tolerance. I go to a friend of mine, Mr. T, who always has beer. Mr. T is the dad of TT, who turned in the fake score that saved my tennis scholarship back in 1989. I grab two beers and chug them. I go back to the match; my nerves are gone. I played perfect and we win the third set easy.

Right after the Norman open tennis tournament I decided to quit Club Quail because of Frank's death. I moved to Mexico City where the Mexican Twins, JO and PO, lived. I was their assistant coach at Oklahoma Christian University. I was trying to get a job teaching tennis anywhere on the beach in Mexico. The Mexican Twins' dad was a top general in the Mexican army. He was good friends with the president of Mexico. I went with five thousand in cash to one of the deadliest cities in the world. The first thing I did when I moved to Mexico City was I went on the hunt for a wild Mexican doctor. I got a script for Valium and painkillers. One morning the general told me that he has a personal bodyguard that drives him everywhere.

His bodyguard was going to take me anywhere I wanted for the day. The Mexican Twins told me to go to the pyramids outside of Mexico City. It was eight AM and I asked the bodyguard to go to a store. All I wanted was a diet coke. He goes in the store and comes out with a twelve pack of beer. He said, "Don't tell anyone, let's get wild." The bodyguard had a day away from the general. Before we made it to the pyramids we killed the twelve pack. There were thousands of tourists all over the pyramids. We looked at the pyramids for one minute and turned around. We didn't give a crap, we just wanted to party.

We went to a cantina a hundred yards from the pyramids.

The jungle was twenty yards right behind us. We kept drinking beer and doing tequila shots at nine AM. I saw an old Mexican man walk out of the jungle. He had a Prestone antifreeze jug. The old Mexican dude was trying to sell us something in the jug. It was something called tepache. I don't know if I'm spelling it right, but its real. The old Mexican dude made it in the jungle. I found out the next day that it was fermented poop and piss. We take a shot each of the tepache for a cultural thing. The only way I would drink something made in the jungle out of a Prestone antifreeze jug was because I was pounding beer and Tequila at nine AM.

The bodyguard is in his army uniform with a loaded 45. He had an ID card that said he was the general's personal bodyguard. He can do almost anything he wants. The Mexican army has way more power than the police. Now the general's bodyguard is my bodyguard. Now my bodyguard is taking off his uniform. I bought a Mexican sombrero at the cantina, and he was wearing it. After the cantina he takes me to another one in Mexico City. He's driving eighty miles an hour everywhere. At the cantina no one was there. Just one Mexican lady closing up. I asked the lady if I could put in my mixed tape in the cantina's stereo. She put my mixed tape in full blast. It had The Cult, Reverend Horton Heat, and Depeche Mode.

We were drinking hard again, and the lady told us she's closing. My bodyguard told her we were staying. She called someone to help her get us out. Three Mexican dudes show up. Then my bodyguard pulls out his 45. He shows them his ID card and they left. I was freaking out telling him to chill out. Then two cops show up with shotguns. I start walking out the back. My bodyguard shows the police his ID card. He's cussing them out and the cops left. I thought I was going to be involved in a gun fight in Mexico City. The lady working was crying; she thought she was going to die. I yell at my bodyguard to get me home right now.

He had to do what I wanted, and we finally go. I gave the

lady working a hundred dollars and said I was sorry. She thanked me for getting my bodyguard out of her bar. On the way back to the general's house it was raining hard. My bodyguard is driving seventy miles an hour hydroplaning. While Reverend Horton Heat was playing full blast on the tape deck.

I'm screaming slow down. He looks like the devil wearing a Mexican sombrero. My bodyguard is screaming at the top of his lungs and goes faster. I was getting ready for a horrible car crash. All I could do was pray. Thank God we got back to the general's alive. When we got back everybody is wondering why we were late. I looked at my friends, the Mexican Twins. I tell them the truth; that I almost died today. The general tells me to go to bed. Now, my bodyguard is the general's bodyguard again. Thank God! The general yells at his bodyguard for an hour. I'm upstairs drunker than hell thinking there's no way this could get worse. I had a horrible case of bacteria from the tepache in the jungle. One of the Mexican Twins, PO, took me to the army hospital ER. They put me on antibiotics and pills for stomach cramps. After that psychotic experience I was ready to move back to OKC, Oklahoma.

When I got back to OKC I got a job teaching tennis at Club Santa. I'm back at the tennis club. I started back in 1990 making sandwiches. It's wild; now I'm working for Aussie OKC. I'm running their junior tennis program. Their junior tennis program was hurting. I give it all I have.

Right when I start working at Club Santa in 1998 I got my second DUI. I was drinking in Norman at the Mont on Thanksgiving. We were leaving the Mont to go to a friend's house for an after party. We were about to leave the parking lot. I got on top of my car and started dancing and yelling. A Norman police officer enjoyed my little dance. He pulled me over instantly and I didn't have a chance. I went to Norman jail for two days for Thanksgiving.

Right after my DUI, a friend of mine talked me into buying a worthless duplex. It had a terrible foundation, and everything was wrong with it. This guy told me he would rebuild the place. And he was going to live on one side of the duplex for free. It got more expensive than we thought, and he bailed. I can't believe I bought that crap hole for eighteen thousand. I was spending my inheritance at a record pace. I saved money on rent and moved into my barn duplex. It was down to bare beams, no windows, no air, no water, no electricity, and a leaky roof. And it had wild animals crawling around like cats and myself.

The OKC police would come by all the time. They told me I can't live here. I showed them my deed paid in full. I told them I'm living here no matter what. Every night after teaching tennis at Club Santa I would go down to the corner liquor store and buy a twelve pack of beer. I was eating Valium like they were candy. I had a Valium connection forever and a high tolerance.

One night I was sitting on my porch drinking and playing Motorhead's greatest hits. I had a loud ghetto blaster with batteries. A Black street hustler was walking down my street. I asked him if he wanted a beer and he sat down. We started partying, then he asks me if I wanted to smoke crack. I gave the dude a hundred dollars and he said he would be right back.

I knew he probably wasn't coming back. He came back and we smoked crack. The second I took one hit I was addicted. I told him to come by every day around seven o'clock. I still had about fifteen thousand dollars left from my dad. I started to smoke crack every day. I hated life when my dad died. Alcohol, Valium, and crack put me in another dimension of euphoria. Now my best friend is a Black street hustler. I even got to know his wife. His wife would cook dinner while we were cracking it up.

My every day was running the junior tennis program at Club Santa, then going to my barn duplex, drinking, and cracking it up. On nights when it would rain I would move my bed around to get away from the leaks. There was a big hole in my floor at my barn duplex. I would get wasted and forget it was there. At night I fell into the hole a couple times up to my waist. I hurt and scared the crap out of me.

At the time I was dating a girl that was a member of Club Santa. I'll call her Coo Coo Clock. We were supposedly in love and talking marriage. One day Coo Coo Clock confessed something to me: that she's never been faithful to her ex-husband or a boyfriend in her life. And she's bisexual. Then she asks me, if I wanted to have a three way with a girlfriend of hers. I'm in shock and tell her no. But I did tell her thanks for being honest because now we're not getting married. She started cheating on me and finally dumped me. She's coo coo for cocoa puffs. I was emotionally like a sixteen-year-old from drinking and drugging since I was sixteen. I lived in my barn duplex cracking it up while trying to get over her. Blasting crack is the worst way to get over a woman.

When my relationships go bad with a woman I feel like it's the end of the world. This is proof of my madness. I quit Club Santa over Coo Coo Clock. I couldn't stand seeing her at my work every day. Aussie OKC, was pissed off and couldn't believe I quit over a woman. I spent a month in an absolute drug haze trying to get her out of my head. After I got over her, I was ready to face the world. Now that I'm writing my book. I was driving my tennis bosses mad because I went back to Club Quail to teach for Redneck. I was so addicted to crack. I started bringing my crack pipe to work with me. I kept my little baggie of crack in my sock while teaching all day. After every lesson, I would run off to get high and come right back.

Chapter Fourteen

1998 Jennifer Miller Starts Drug Overdosing / The Tennis Pro Am

Destruction and misery are in their paths.

—Romans 3:16

–Shitlist, L7

Craig Miller was done with drugs and alcohol for life. There was no turning back for him. He was getting his degree from seminary and living for God. Susan and Cool Dude had a baby girl. Susan and Cool Dude's baby girl's name is Sassy C. They are living in the Woodlands, Texas. Mary quit smoking cigarettes and stayed sober for life. Jennifer almost died a few times from drug overdoses. Jennifer had so many drug overdoses that I couldn't keep track.

One night Jennifer was shooting up heroin in a Pizza Hut parking lot in OKC. She started her car and went for a drive. She almost hit the pizza hut front doors. The cops came fast and they took her to the hospital. The police, paramedic, and hospital saved her life. Another OD Jennifer took a massive number of pills. She decided to go for a drive on the highway. She pulled into Tinker Airforce Base in Midwest City, Oklahoma. She thought Tinker Airforce Base was a toll gate. Jennifer drove up to the armed guards and threw change at them. She was yelling at them to let her drive through.

They took her out of her car and called the police. The

paramedics took her to the hospital and saved her life. After this OD Jennifer went to a women's prison in Texas for six months. After prison she was going to AA meetings. Jennifer would get some good months of sobriety and relapse. When Jennifer was sober, she was my favorite woman to hang out with. When she was high, she turned into a psychotic witch. For example, Jennifer was doing well with a good chunk of sobriety. One night I go to her house to hang out. She is wasted on pills and falling all over the place. When she went to the bathroom, and I went through her purse, I found her pills and took them. Jennifer knows I took them and grabs a butter knife from the kitchen. She says give me my Valium or I'm going to kill you. I'm not going to give them back. Jennifer could OD and die. She comes at me with the butter knife. I grab an old tennis racquet laying around. Her and I are at war and I'm laughing at her butter knife. I'm blocking her butter knife thrust with her old racquet. I'm kicking her butt and she gives up. I take her car keys and run out the door. Here's my addiction and hypocrisy kicking in. I go out that night and start eating her Valium. That night the band L7 played at VZDs in OKC. Cocky, Sarah, and I went to the show. Cocky being Cocky lights up a joint and we smoked it in VZDs. We were lucky to see L7 in a small bar. I come back the next day to give Jennifer her car keys back. I come in and she punches me in the nose. I run to my car and peel out. You do not want to be on Jennifer Millers shitlist. I stayed away from her for a while. One day she calls me and wants to hang out. She's been sober for a couple weeks. Junior Brown was playing that night in brick town. He's one of the best guitar players in the world. Jenny and I had a great sober time that night. We hung out a lot when we were both sober. When people say I'm only hurting myself by abusing drugs, that's a lie. Your family and loved ones are going through it with you.

I'm still living in my barn duplex and teaching tennis at Club Quail. One night in my barn duplex I was hammered drunk and cracking it up. I had a group lesson with a bunch of kids at eight AM. That night I fell in my hole in the floor again. I raked my shins on the side of the hole and was bleeding. I went out my front door and put my hand into a rusty nail. My hand was bleeding. I wrapped my t-shirt around my hand tight. Then I drank warm beer and passed out.

That morning I got up around eight AM. I went to the pay phone at the corner liquor store. I called Redneck and said I had the flu. He told me to get my butt up there or I'm fired. I blew in my cars breathalyzer and it wouldn't start. DUI breathalyzers will not start your car if you have alcohol in your system. I'm late and a group of kids are waiting on me. I go next door to a neighbor, and he blows in my breathalyzer. The car started and I went to work. By the time I got to work the kids left. I have a t-shirt wrapped around my hand. Redneck made me go clean up and work all day.

All I could think about was smoking crack that night. I would get so paranoid on crack in my barn duplex. When I heard the slightest noise I thought it was the whole OKC police force coming to take me to jail. I would go down my big whole in my floor. Crawl under the floor in the dirt or mud. Then hide for about an hour and calm down a little. Then go back up and take a bunch more hits. I would hear a noise again and go back under the floor. Then repeat that madness all night long. The police were never after me.

Redneck and his wife offered me to move into their guest home. They knew I was living in a barn duplex. They didn't know what I was doing in my barn duplex. They cared about me, and I love them for that. I wasn't going to give up my massive drug habit. My job at Club Quail started going downhill fast.

I've learned in AA. It's good to remember your horrible past of addiction. If you forget your horrible drug past and get cocky you most definitely will go back to using drugs. I was good friends with a member at Club Quail. He played football for the University of Oklahoma. He won a national title in the mid-fifties at quarterback. He wanted me to house sit for him. While I was house sitting, there was a massive pro-am doubles tour at Club Quail.

Redneck was gone playing a tournament in another state. The next pro in line was running the pro-am. I played as an amateur with a cool Black pro from Kansas. That weekend we played a crapload of eight game pro sets. It was a round robin draw and we were beating everyone. I was doing all my drugs hard all weekend. We get to the semifinals of the pro-am. I haven't slept in two days. When I'm tired I'm not nervous. I don't think, I hit the ball as hard as possible. In the finals we were playing a great team. The pro is from Spain and won a team national title for OCU. He was their number one player. He had crazy top spin on everything. His serve was insane, it kicked like a kangaroo. The Spaniard's armature was WH, a sixty-plus-year-old member at Club Quail. He was a great tennis player and loved to party.

The match was close; we lost six to eight in the finals. WH asked me to go upstairs to the bar. The pro running the pro-am came to the bar. He told me to get back to work. I was so tired and told him no. He told me when Redneck comes back I'm fired. When Redneck came back from his tournament, I wasn't in trouble. After the pro-am I couldn't maintain my drug abuse anymore. I finally gave up and quit Club Quail for good. Everybody at Club Quail was glad I was leaving.

Chapter Fifteen

2000 The New Millennium / The Bank Robbery

Whoever utters the name of the lord must be put to death. The whole community must stone him whether alien or native. If he utters the name, he must be put to death.

—Leviticus 24:16

–Dance of the Mad Bastards, Pop Will Eat Itself

OU football wins a national title and I quit listing to new music. All I cared about was my drug addiction. I just kept listening to music from my past and dwelling on it. People have asked me, what my relationships with people were like. My relationships with people back then sucked. My true love and relationship were with drugs and alcohol. I was extremely selfish; I didn't give a crap about anyone but myself and drugs. Aussie OKC hired me back at Club Santa. I'm still living in my barn duplex and it's getting cold out. I'm wearing a lot of clothes, two sleeping bags, and boots to bed. At bedtime, I drank hard and pass out. And hoped I didn't freeze to death.

One night it was freezing and it's snowing through my window. I couldn't take living in that freezing barn duplex anymore. I finally sold my barn duplex for crack money. I moved in with an old friend from Norman High, class of 1985. I introduced

Mad Bastard to the madness of crack. Oh, by the way Mad Bastard has a wife. I'm living on their living room floor. We are cracking it up all night every night while his wife is in the next room freaking out. Mad Bastard's wife leaves him and moves out.

Mad Bastard goes crazy and starts stealing from his work for crack. I smoked my barn duplex money. I started to steal from Club Santa for crack money. I was taking cash from tennis lessons and putting it in my pocket. There were nights when Mad Bastard would attack me for no reason. He kept attacking me, so we started a two-man fight club. We beat the crap out of each other. When you're a hardcore crack head and you run out of crack, the logical thing to do is drink all the alcohol in the house and fight.

One day Mad Bastard pawned my TV and VCR for crack. He told the truth and apologized. I wasn't mad, I just wanted crack, but he already smoked it. Then I got mad and moved out. I moved into another apartment for a while. I haven't heard from Mad Bastard in four or five months. One night I just got off the court teaching tennis at Club Santa and the front desk tells me I have a phone call. Mad Bastard is on the other line and yells, "Fight club!" I'm still mad at him for pawning my stuff. He tells me, he has the five hundred bucks he owes me. He tells me, he has two thousand dollars' worth of crack. I can't turn down crack. I go pick him up at a strip bar. He gives me five hundred bucks and shows me the most crack I've ever seen. We get two cases of beer and go back to my apartment.

Mad Bastard keeps peeking out my window all night. He's making me paranoid. I asked him where he got all this money. He keeps saying you don't want to know. He finally tells me that he is a crack dealer. That made sense so I left him alone. We're up all night and there's still way too much crack. I had to go teach tennis. I tell Mad Bastard he can stay here. I came home from work and he's long gone. I go to bed; I haven't slept in a while.

That morning I get a call from my friend Cocky. He says,

do you know what happened to Mad Bastard. He robbed a bank with a squirt gun in his coat pocket. He robbed the bank in the student union at OU. Mad Bastard was all over the news and he didn't even wear a disguise. It might look like I had something to do with the bank robbery. I call the police and they tell me to call the FBI.

I'm talking to the FBI, and I tell the truth. The FBI agent asked me where Mad Bastard was. I told him I didn't know. He asked me if I have the five hundred bucks. I spent it on rent that morning. The FBI agent believed me. I didn't have to give the five hundred back. The FBI agent told me that I'm not in trouble. They have all my information. They will get back with me if they have more questions.

I almost crapped my pants I was so scared. The next day Mad Bastard calls me. He is in a hotel room, and he is going to die from a heart attack. I told him to call his mom to come get him and turn himself in. He did that and he went to prison. Mad Bastard told the FBI that I had nothing to do with the bank robbery. I was hurt bad about my friend going to prison. I introduced him to crack, one of the most insane drugs of all time. Maybe that is what he needed to hit bottom and get help. I wasn't ready to give up crack yet. Crack is a bleeding nightmare strait from hell.

Chapter Sixteen

2001 September 11th – 911 / Eric Visits the Nut House

Babylon has been a golden cup in the hand of the lord, intoxicating all the earth. The nations have drunk of her wine; Therefore, the nations are going mad.

—Jeremiah 51:7

–Human Fly, The Cramps

I went to a friend JS's house one night to party. In the morning he tells me to watch the news. I was hungover and told him to leave me alone. When I got up 911 was on TV. I thought it was the end of the world. I was already paranoid twenty-four-seven from crack, and snorting coke. I started freaking members out at Club Santa, with my end of the world talk. I moved again into a one room apartment off sixty-third street in OKC. I couldn't afford my other place.

My main crack dealer that I used since my dad died was a big bad Black dude with a gold tooth. I called him The Man and he called me Tennis Boy. The Man had a small crew of mean Black dudes. It probably was a scary place to go to. When you must have your crack it's normal. The Man lived right by Classen and thirty-sixth street in OKC.

The Man played tennis with his crew at the park. He was a beginner and liked tennis a lot. I would go to the tennis courts at the park to get crack sometimes. Then I would stay and play The Man in tennis. I wasn't just stealing money from Club Santa. I would take Prince tennis shoes from the pro shop. I would trade The Man for crack. I even took a Prince tennis racquet and traded it. The Man looked like a pro tennis player on the tour. After he had too much tennis gear The Man only wanted "green," as he would call money. My drug abuse was so bad that I couldn't teach tennis anymore. I quit Club Santa again. I know what you're thinking, I've quit more tennis jobs than anyone in the country. I honestly don't know why any of my bosses hired me back. Now I wasn't working and broke. I couldn't afford drugs anymore. I couldn't even afford cheap beer.

I sat in my apartment waiting to be evicted. I had a notice on my door to get out in a week. A couple days later I was curled up in the fetal position. I'm screaming bloody murder withdrawing off drugs. Craig knocked on my door telling me he was taking me to the crisis center. I wouldn't answer and he climbed in my window. Craig helps me to my mom's car. They took me to the crisis center in OKC. I signed my name on the bottom line. That means I'm staying there until the man says go. The crisis center in OKC, is a detox center and mental health center.

I'm being detoxed of drugs and on suicide watch. We are locked in there like jail. People in the crisis center are suicidal, violent, drug addicts, alcoholics, and mentally ill. I'm on suicide watch in a room with another dude. This dude was strapped to his bed with restraints. He was huge and reminded me of a shaggy haired Frankenstein's monster. We were the only two dudes in our room on suicide watch. Frankenstein was trying to break out of his straps. It was scaring the crap out of me. Then for some reason the staff thought Frankenstein was okay. They let him out of his straps. That night Frankenstein gets up and walks right up to my bed. Then he starts digging through my clothes. I yelled, "Frankenstein is trying to kill me!"

The staff comes running in to our room and puts Frankenstein back in his straps. I'm begging the staff to get me out of the room. The staff ask me if I was still feeling suicidal. I told them no and please get me out of this room now. The staff puts me in another room with a guy that's literally psychotic. The staff told me not to get mad at him because he had no idea what was going on. This dude's eyes were wide open and staring at me constantly. I told him to quit looking at me. He didn't even know I was there. He freaked me out; I couldn't sleep. I told the staff that I need to sleep or I'm going to attack my roommate. The staff finally put me in my own room. Now it's time to have fun at the nut house.

When fights would break out dudes would get taken down by the staff. The staff kept shooting something in their butt to calm them down. Then putting them in the padded cell in a strait jacket. I started asking the staff what drug were they shooting in their butt? The staff kept telling me to shut up. One day these two dudes were wanting out of the crisis center. They didn't realize they signed on the bottom line on the paperwork that they can't leave until the man says go. These two dudes started planning their escape, and I heard every word. Their plan was hilarious and wasn't going to work.

One of the dudes climbed into the air conditioning vent in his room. He started crawling through and was stuck. I told the staff he was stuck. The staff grabbed him and pulled him out of the air conditioning vent. The dude attacked the staff and they shot him up with the mystery drug. They put him in a strait jacket in the padded cell. If you physically attack the staff, they call the police. This dude was taken to jail.

I asked a nurse what the mystery drug was. She told me its liquid Valium. I started planning to get the shot in my butt. Valium is one of my favorite drugs on the planet. I wanted a relaxing trip to the padded cell in a strait jacket. I purposely started a fight with one of the staff. I didn't touch the staff. I just got really loud and crazy. The staff put me in a bear hug. They didn't bring the shot of Valium. I asked the staff where's the shot. The staff figured out I was just trying to get Valium. I was lucky and wasn't taken to jail.

The staff were getting tired of me messing with them. The staff wanted me out bad. When the psychiatrist told me I was being released I told him that I wanted to stay in the crisis center forever. After being in the crisis center for two weeks my bro Craig takes me to live with him. I didn't make it a couple of days. I was right back in the drug race. At the time I joined a 4.0 men's USTA tennis team. My captain was one of my dad's best friends. Our 4.0 team went to the next level for the Oklahoma title. The 4.0 tournament was at the biggest outdoor tennis center in OKC. One 4.0 team we were playing was from Stillwater, Oklahoma. Stillwater's best 4.0 singles player was way too good for a 4.0. This dude was a 5.0 level. 5.0 was beating our best 4.0 singles player as bad as possible. 5.0 was playing with his nondominate hand and killing our guy. 5.0 was making fun of our guy for no reason. Our guy was the nicest dude on our team. During the match I exploded on 5.0. I went on the court and threatened him. Then the captain for Stillwater yelled at me to shut up. I went to the captain's court and told him to come on with it. My team was trying to get me to chill out and go home. I finally left, then I went home and got drunk and smoked crack. Cracked out of my mind, I called a bunch of my teammates and apologized. Welcome to the madness of drug addiction.

Craig was an associate pastor at our church in OKC, near tenth and Western. I'm apologizing in advance for my actions at church. Craig was commuting back and forth to Southwestern Baptist Seminary in Fort Worth, Texas. Craig and I lived down the street from our church. After the nut house I got my job back at Club Santa. I was teaching tennis and running the junior program. Aussie OKC didn't know I was in the nut house. I tried to hide my drug abuse. No one really knew what I was doing. Obviously I was doing a good job for the tennis clubs I worked for. Or I would have been fired a long time ago and banned from teaching tennis in OKC for life.

91

Chapter Seventeen

2004 Living in the Woods with the Devil

The wicked go down to the realm of the dead, all the nations that forgot God.

—Psalm 9:17

–Crackin Up, Rev Co.

I don't know about you people reading my book. I'm getting tired of talking about crack. I'm sorry about all the crack talk, but it's a massive part of my life. I'm living with Craig down the street from our church. He caught me smoking crack a couple times. Craig told me, if I don't stop he's kicking me out. I couldn't quit, now I'm homeless. I had a brilliant idea and bought a one-man green camouflage tent. I wanted to live in the woods on Club Santa's property. I ask Aussie OKC if I could camp out there for a while. I told him camping sounds fun and I haven't done it in a while. He thought it was an odd request, but he let me move into the woods.

I'm living in the woods next to the outdoor tennis courts. My luxurious tent had a battery alarm clock and my battery ghetto blaster. The Man would bring me crack every night to Club Santa's parking lot. Then I would walk across the street to get my twelve pack of beer. I would crack it up in my tent every night. One Sunday I went to my church to talk to Craig. I was going to kill myself that day. Craig was working and church was about to start. He came out to the parking lot really quick. I asked what it says in the bible about killing myself. Will I go to hell? Craig told me if you kill yourself, do you want to risk it. I had just enough faith in God. It stopped me from doing it. That made me mad I had to keep going.

Crack gave me little euphoria and extreme paranoia in my chronic use years. Living in the woods on crack was a nightmare. God wasn't there, I was running from God. I didn't want to think about my horrible life at all. As a matter of fact, Satan was down in those woods with me. Satan was loving every minute of it.

Enough of this depressing crap, let's have a laugh. One night in the woods I had just taken a couple big fat hits of crack. I heard a growling and chirping noise. I look out the tent zipper and see two small animals. This wasn't a hallucination; they were real. I take a stick and throw it at them. They weren't scared and they came a couple feet closer. I throw another stick at them. They came a couple more feet closer. They were two pissed off skunks.

I didn't know what to do. I thought they were going to spray me or give me rabies. I slowly get out of the tent and close the zipper. I run up the hill to Club Santa's upstairs deck. These two little grumpy skunks were right behind me. I'm upstairs on the deck with the skunks below chirping and growling. Those two little warriors wanted me bad.

I'm on the deck and theirs a camera recording everything I'm doing. I think the police are coming, because I'm very paranoid. All the sudden I realize, my crack is down in the tent. I need a hit right now. I have to go back to the tent. I go for it running downhill and the skunks are right behind me. I jumped in my tent and zipped it. I was blasting crack while the skunks were trying to scratch through the tent. I'm up all night and freaking out.

During the day after teaching a tennis lesson I made a spear from a tree. I was going to kill my first animal. It would have been in self-defense. That night the skunks come to my tent ready for war. I was lucky they didn't try to spray me down. I can't kill an animal and never used my spear. Partying all night with the skunks, I finally figured something out. I was in the skunk's territory, and they weren't going away. I woke up the next morning and moved my tent deeper in the woods. Those warrior skunks left me alone. I missed my skunk friends because they distracted me from wanting to die.

After the skunks I was still in the tent for a month. I started talking to God again and asked for help. I asked God to get me off all drugs for a week. I was going through wicked withdrawals and still teaching tennis. I made it and called a men's sober living home in OKC. The sober men's living home took me in. A good friend of mine, I taught all his kids' tennis, took me to the men's home and paid my first week's rent. He's a great dude, I thought nobody gave a crap.

I moved into the sober men's home. It was a big house in a good neighborhood. The new guys slept two to a room. We had weekly meetings and drug tests. The drug tests are called UAs and you pee in a cup. If we had any alcohol or drugs in our system we were kicked out and homeless. We were assigned jobs and chores like the president, vice president, chore coordinator, buying supplies, and more. The guys that were their the longest, were president and vice president. They had their own room. The more sobriety you had the more responsibility you got. Living there was a great sober life. Everybody at Club Santa and my family were very happy with me. I was feeling reborn, and life was great again. Thank you God, for getting me out of the woods from hell.

Chapter Eighteen

2005 New Life / Men's Sober Living Home

Be strong and courageous. Do not be afraid or terrified because of them, for the Lord your God goes with you, he will never leave you nor forsake you.

—Deuteronomy 31:6

–Long Way Back from Hell, Danzig

I'm sober for the first time in a long time. I'm kicking butt at Club Santa and playing a ton of tennis again. My sister Susan and Cool Dude were still living in the Woodlands, Texas with their kids. My sister Jennifer was going to AA and having good chunks of sobriety. My brother Craig was still sober and preaching God's word. Craig is my mentor; we hung out constantly. I came clean with Aussie OKC. I admitted I stole money from him for a couple years from the pro shop and putting money in my pocket.

Aussie OKC told me that after admitting I stole from him he now respected me more than ever. I also paid him back in full eventually. I never admitted smoking crack in the woods. He just thought I was having fun camping. With my new sobriety my running the junior tennis program and playing tennis was better. I joined a USTA 8.0 mixed doubles league in OKC. Our teams went to the next level a couple times. I was a good 4.0 or an average 4.5 level.

Right when things were going so well my addiction came back. I started cracking it up. Drug addiction is always eating at you. The men's sober living home had a drug test every Sunday. I knew when I could smoke crack. It leaves your system in three days. Yes, in a sober living home I started doing drugs again. It was every once and awhile not every day. Some other guys in our home were still doing drugs. One guy was dealing cocaine out of our sober living home. I didn't know this at the time, or I would have gotten it from him.

At the time Jennifer was living with my mom. One day my mom Mary calls me up. Mary tells me, Jennifer hasn't been home in three days and she's crying. I told my mom Jennifer is an adult and she's an addict. She will come home when she's had enough. That's exactly what my mom was worried about. Jennifer's enough could be death. I became a detective and made a couple phone calls.

One of Jennifer's friends knew where she was. She was with some creepy meth dealer in Norman. I got the meth dealers telephone number from her friend. I called him and told him I was Jennifer's brother. I told him I come in peace, and I just wanted to talk to her. He gave the phone to Jennifer. I asked her if she wanted to come back to Mom's. She gave me the address and I drove to Norman. I was lucky this meth dealer wasn't a violent gun-toting madman. If he was, I would have died for Jennifer. I put Jennifer in my car and drove to OKC. She hasn't slept for a long time and was hallucinating. Driving Jennifer back to OKC was scary. She was talking madness and seemed possessed. Jennifer was back at Mom's and went to bed. My mom was very happy.

The next day Jennifer woke up and disappeared. Mary calls me again and wants Jennifer back. I go back to Norman and this time I'm pissed off. You must understand that everybody in the meth dealer's house hadn't slept in forever and was extremely paranoid. My plan is to act like I'm the police to freak everyone out. I'm at the meth house and peek in the front window. I see Jennifer and everyone in the house are women. I pounded on the door yelling, "This is the police, open up!" I was watching in the window. I could see everybody running around freaking out. Stashing illegal stuff and running out the back.

Jennifer came to the door ready to fight the police. She immediately knew it was me. She punched me in the nose and I was bleeding. If Jennifer didn't smoke cigarettes or do drugs she could have been a professional fighter. I was blocking her punches and trying to chill her out. She told everyone in the house, "It's not the police, it's my *blanking* brother." She wasn't coming home, so I left. I told my mom that Jennifer is an adult. If she doesn't want to stop using drugs we must leave her alone.

At my sober men's home everybody was out of control. A lot of the dudes where doing whatever they wanted. I couldn't take it anymore and wanted sobriety. I moved into another men's sober house. I couldn't get away with doing drugs or drinking. Dudes were getting kicked out constantly. They gave random drug tests. I stopped smoking crack and stayed sober for real. You could have women in your room to visit. Dudes were humping like wild dogs. This house was about to get greasy.

We had to live with two or three dudes jammed in a room. One night I was asleep and a guy brought a stripper into our room. They started having sex right next to me in his bed. I woke up and yelled at them. I told them what is wrong with you freaks. I went to the living room to sleep. That guy was facing fifteen years in prison for selling meth. He wouldn't stop humping girls in our room. I declared war on greasy meth man and complained to the house. The house didn't care; they all were humping like wild dogs. There's one thing about sobriety: People switch addictions and sex is a big one.

One day I caught greasy meth man humping on my bed. Why my bed? I wanted to wrestle him, but he literally had oil on him. I wasn't completely innocent in our fight. I always ate his Rocky Road ice cream. He never knew it was me. After a while, greasy meth man didn't sleep for a week. The house drug tested him, and he was kicked out. The junior tennis program I started at Club Santa exploded. It turned into a massive and talented program. I was in the sober living homes for two years. I finally saw what being sober was like. It was ten times better than what I was doing before. Then my addiction comes back like a sneaky demon. I was caught on a drug test on Valium and kicked out. I moved into a friend's house from church. I started cracking it up, drinking, and popping pills again. Addiction is exhausting!

Chapter Nineteen

The Insanity of Drug and Alcohol Abuse

Heal me, lord, and I will be healed. Save me and I will be saved, for you are the one I praise.

—Jeremiah 17:14

—Research Chemicals, Viagra Boys

Addiction is a self-destructive nightmare. I truly think that a lot of people abuse drugs to numb their mental pain. Something in their life hurt them bad to where they don't want to think or deal with it. It's easier to take drugs to numb the pain in your brain then deal with it in the correct way. The second I was kicked out of the men's sober living home I could do whatever I wanted. There was no more accountability. I went right back to drinking and drugging.

At Club Santa, I tried hiding my crack use from everyone. I was smoking crack everywhere at Club Santa like closets, backdrops behind the courts, in the back room of the pro shop, and bathrooms. People would walk in on me and ask, "What are you doing in here?" I would tell them, "I don't know what you're talking about." I was borrowing money from a couple teaching pros at work. I was borrowing money at late hours; when they were home with their families. I made up legitimate reasons why I needed the money right now. I would go to their house, cracked out of my mind, and get the money, then go buy my crack. I was hunting for crack in bad areas of OKC because my dealer The Man disappeared. I would drive around my neighborhood in the ghetto. I would find the most obvious crack house. I didn't know any of these wild animals. I would go right up to the porch and get it.

One night at that crack house the police were in the street waiting for people to leave and pull them over. My car is in the street in front of the crack house. A cop is right behind my car checking out my tags. The police obviously know who I am. A lady that ran the crack house told us, "Don't leave, wait for the cops to go away." I thought I was going to jail. I was smoking my crack waiting for the police to go away. The police were out front for two hours, it was a nightmare. I still went back to that crack house with the police watching it constantly. Another time at the same crack house there was a Black crack dealer. His street name was LA. I gave LA eighty dollars to get me crack. He told me he would be right back; he never came back. A couple days later I pull up to the crack house. LA is out front wasted, drinking vodka. I get in his face wanting my crack. I wanted my crack so bad; I was willing to die. Thank God, LA was drunk and in a good mood. LA gave me my eighty bucks in crack, and we partied all day.

During that time Jennifer had another drug overdose that I haven't mentioned in the book until now. She ate a mix of painkillers and downers. A friend of hers went in her house and found her. She was admitted into a hospital where a friend of mine was her doctor. He was a squash member at Club Santa, and I taught his kid tennis. Jennifer had a twenty percent chance of living. She had a bad staph infection and was on kidney dialysis. We were getting prepared for her death. All the sudden she made it out alive.

Right before that OD Jennifer got her biology degree from the University of Central Oklahoma in Edmond. She had a great job working for the state in a laboratory. Even with all this great stuff happening in her life she still OD.

This is a fact, very few people stay sober after they go to a drug treatment center for the first time. A lot of the people are forced to go to treatment. They obviously did not want sobriety. I've had so many friends get out of treatment, and party the same day.

My brother Craig was getting married to a beautiful woman from our church. Craig asked me to be his best man and I did. I've never been asked to be anyone's best man before. The night before the rehearsal I had an all-nighter on multiple drugs. I couldn't wake up for the rehearsal. He took another friend to be his best man. I showed up for the wedding at our church. I spent more time sneaking around the church smoking crack then attending my brother's wedding. I show up right before their wedding vows, cracked out of my mind.

That's what crack addicts do; we always need a hit right now. What I'm about to admit to you could be one of the definitions of the insanity of drug abuse. A couple times, I would be cracking it up way too hard. One time I took a bunch of hits. I fell to the ground paralyzed with chest pains. I thought I was dying of a heart attack. I was praying to God to take me to heaven right now. The second I could move again, and my chest pains were gone, I would take a couple more hits and fall to the ground again. That happened so many times, but I kept doing it.

Drug addicts do insane things to get their next fix. Drug addicts commit murder, sell their bodies, and other things I can't comprehend. Prisons are overcrowded with drug addicts with drug offenses. I hate to say this, but drug addiction is never going away. This is my opinion. The best way you can prevent drug addiction is parents must be extremely careful not to do drugs or drink alcohol around their children. Alcohol and drugs are the same, they're both chemicals. I'm not judging anyone, but if you are chemically dependent your kids have a great chance to be chemically dependent. That's one of the reasons why I never had children. Oh, by the way alcohol, tobacco, and sugar kill more people a year than all illegal drugs combined. Illegal drugs are a joke compared to legal drugs. Most Americans are in denial about this fact. Because most of America are doing these legal drugs. Its all-total insanity!

Chapter Twenty

2007 The End of a Great Junior Tennis Program

The Lord is close to the brokenhearted and saves those who are crushed in spirit.

—Psalm 34:18

—Isolation, Joy Division

Back to my life after being kicked out of my sober men's home. I just moved in with a friend from church. My friend from church is sober for twenty years. I'm living in one of his bedrooms hiding my crack use. At the time I'm riding a yellow moped everywhere. At Club Santa things were rocking. I was running the show with two great assistants. They were both national champions in college tennis and great teaching pros. I was trying to hide my addiction from everyone. I was in the chronic stages of it. Crack made me extremely paranoid and scared. I was already feeling like when I was living in the woods.

I was showing up late to my own program cracked out of my mind. I was borrowing money late night to smoke crack from a couple of pros that worked at Club Santa that I mentioned in chapter nineteen. My assistants were getting tired of my crap. One day my assistants went to Aussie OKC, and we all had a meeting. My junior tennis program was taken from me. I don't blame them.

I wasn't fired and was still teaching tennis at Club Santa. I was teaching the junior beginner groups. That's what I was best at anyways. I wasn't mad at all, and my stress was gone. During the junior program when I was still in charge, I kicked a dad out of my program, and he didn't do anything wrong, because I was out of my mind on crack, and paranoid. His boy was top five in America in ten and under. His whole family are great people. I now feel bad about what happened. I apologize to you and your family with all my heart. If you're reading this book, I hope to God, you can forgive me. I would love to talk about 80's new wave bands again.

I'm trying once again to get sober. I rented a four-bedroom house on tenth street in OKC. My church and I turned it into a Christian men's sober living home. I lived there and ran it. I had about four guys always living there. We all had to follow the rules and go to church on Sundays. I was still cracking it up every once and a while. I let the guys in my house get away with relapsing once. I was still using and didn't want to be a hypocrite. If they weren't being violent I let them stay. When people have been addicted to drugs and alcohol most their lives, how can anybody expect them to get sober their first try. They will be homeless if their kicked out and being homeless is a nightmare. Two of the guys living there were friends of mine.

Life at my sober living home is about to get crazy. One of my friends that lived there started dating my sister Jennifer. One day Jennifer came over to the house wasted and crazy. I told her to leave the house. She called me a hypocrite and punched me in the face again. I wrestled her to the ground. I had one of her friends in AA to come get her. Another day, I heard something weird coming out of my friend's room. I found my sister in his bed without him. I wake her up and ask her why she's here.

She told me my friend and her were smoking crack all night. He borrowed her car and never came back. My friend didn't come back for days. He came back drunk one night and didn't have her car. We were the only people in the house at the time. I ask him, "Where's my sisters' car?" He told me to go *blank* myself. I started asking harder and he kept telling me to *blank* myself.

He hit me hard in the forehead, it almost knocked me out. I remember telling myself, while he was trying to finish me off, to stay awake and block his punches. I snap out of it and wrestled him on his back. I had to hit him in the face repeatedly to knock him out. I had to knock him out so I could call the police. I call the police and open the door. The OKC police showed up in record time.

The police asked me if I wanted to press charges. I told the police that if he tells us where the car is I won't press charges. My friend told the police what happened and that he sold the car for crack. He sold it to a crack house down the street. It wasn't the crack house I was going to. There were a bunch of crack houses in the area. The cops put him in the back of the car and told me to follow. We went to the crack house and the police told me to wait.

The police went to the house and asked where the car was. The crack house said nothing. The police asked me what I wanted to do with my friend. I didn't have him go to jail. I had the cops drop him off wherever he wanted. A week later the police found Jennifer's car with the stereo missing. Jennifer has her car back. After that I never saw my friend again. I hope he's alive and happy. My friend, if you're reading this book, please get ahold of me buddy.

Shortly after that incident Aussie OKC sold Club Santa. He was one of the owners. After all that time Club Santa was history. Everybody that worked there left. Now, I'm not working at all. I started dating a girl that I went to Norman High with. I instantly traded my crack addiction for a woman. My relationships with girlfriends get crazy fast because I'm emotionally like a teenager. After a good while she dumped me and put me out of my misery. One great thing happened from our time together: I never smoked crack or snorted coke again because I went to a doctor in

OKC. I told him that I was in pain from playing tennis. I just wanted to get high and numb my pain from the breakup. The doctor gave me opioid painkillers, Xanax, and some muscle relaxers. This was every month for as long as I wanted. Back then doctors gave you whatever you wanted.

Chapter Twenty-One

The Ghetto Tennis Courts in OKC, Oklahoma

*God never leaves us, we leave God. God is always waiting for us
to come back.*

—Eric Miller

–New Jack Hustler, Ice T

My favorite place in the world to play tennis is at the Ghetto Courts
in OKC, at Goodholm Park. The Ghetto Courts have mainly Black
tennis players there. The Black players are the ones who named it
the Ghetto Courts. Most Black tennis players go all out when they
play tennis.

Meaning, they're very vocal, wild, and crazy like me. I
need players like that. I get bored easy on the tennis court. If you
want tennis war, go to the Ghetto Courts. I was going through some
of the worst times of my life. No matter how crazy I got it never
shocked anyone.

My usual routine at the Ghetto Courts every day was warm
up against the wall. By the time I was warm some warrior wanted
tennis war. I felt like I was playing in the land of the giants. Meaning, really tall dudes and ex pro and college athletes. One of those
dudes is the tallest player I've ever played in tennis. Big E is seven
foot tall and played center in the NBA. His serve came straight

down at you, like it was coming out of a tree. The hard part was blocking the giant out when he's attacking the net. I got used to it by only watching the ball.

The Ghetto Classic Tennis Tournament every year is great tennis. Black tennis players come from all over the country. One year in the Ghetto Classic my partner and I were a good doubles team. We were beaten one and one first round.

I heard a story about one of my Black friends, Big CB, from the Ghetto Courts. One day he was playing friendly doubles. He was playing against a new guy. The new guy threatened to kill everyone on the court. CB went to his van and pulled out his machete. He threatened the homicidal madman with chopping him up. Thank God, no one was hurt that day. CB is a tennis warrior. Never a dull moment at the Ghetto Courts.

A true confession. There is a high-ranking Black DEA agent Big C. C and I played tennis there a lot. Obviously, you know now. I was using a lot of illegal drugs while we were playing. Some of the best teaching pros in OKC, teach at the Ghetto Courts every day. One of them is Big J. J has one of the biggest and best free junior tennis programs in the country. I am honored to have worked for him in his program. Another great teaching pro at the Ghetto Courts is Big Bad L. L was teaching a big up-and-coming Black teenage girl at the time. I was also playing tennis with more cool Black dudes. Their nicknames are Pen, Green Jaguar Man, RC the OU baseball player, and Cool A with the plastic knee. I love everybody at the Ghetto Courts. Thank you for everything. I'll be back for tennis war real soon and I'm not going to lose.

Chapter Twenty-Two

2007 Death of Jennifer Miller / My Encounters with
Famous Pro Tennis Players

My beautiful sister, I can't wait to be with you in heaven, and there
will be no pain.

—Eric Miller

–She's my Sister, Stone Roses

When my little sister Jennifer was raped in the third grade in Vermillion, South Dakota she was on a self-destructive path her whole
life. Jennifer Miller was forty years old and homeless. Nobody in
our family would let her live with them. She could OD any day.
Even if we did let her move in she would have left to use drugs.

One day Jennifer came to visit me. We talked for a while
and she said she was going to Norman, Oklahoma. The last thing
I said to her was please don't die. Jennifer went to an old friend of
hers. Jennifer had fentanyl patches, a crazy strong opioid. Jennifer
put on way too many patches. She put warm towels over the fentanyl patches to get the opioid in her system faster. The next morning the guy found her dead on his couch. This guy is a nice guy
and a great friend of Jennifer. I'm sorry she died on your couch.
Jennifer was going to OD and die. It was just a matter of time. Nobody on the planet could help her or change her. If Jennifer's friend

111

is reading this book, our whole family loves you dude. We don't blame you at all.

My little sister is finally out of her misery. Jennifer was never married or had kids. We had her funeral at our church. There were a lot of people there from AA, friends, family, and the church. I got up and spoke. I said, "I've been punched in the face by Jennifer so many times. I can't keep track. I wish she was alive and here to punch me in the face right now. Jennifer was the funniest and sweetest girl to hang with. Jennifer Miller is finally at peace. I can't wait to hug her in heaven." The day of Jennifer's death, Craig called me. He told me he has bad news and was crying. I said, "Did Jennifer die?" and he said yes. I'll be brutally honest right now, at the time of Jennifer's death I was sad and cried but I was on so many drugs. Drugs numbed my grief and sadness for Jennifer. Now, that I'm writing about her and sober it's making me cry way worse now. I almost couldn't get through this chapter.

My Encounters with Famous Tennis Playing Pros

NUMBER 1: In 1973 this dude played in the battle of the sexes. In 1977 he came to Club Red in Norman, Oklahoma. This pro put on a tennis clinic. He hit with each kid for five minutes. I can say I hit with this dude.

NUMBER 2: Around 1980. Pro team tennis came to OKC. I was a ball boy for it. During one doubles match. I was right behind a cocky South African. He was a pro player in the mid-70's. And a long-time pro tennis commentator. I'm so nervous that I freaked out and toss him a ball right in the middle of his serve motion. The ball hits him in the back. He hits the ball back at me and hits me with it. The crowd booed him big time.

NUMBER 3: After that one. Two legends came to OKC to play an exhibition match. The American was known for his bad temper. The other pro had a massive tennis arm, long hair, and came from Argentina. A friend and I stole one of the tennis shoes from the American. To this day I have no idea where the shoe is.

NUMBER 4: When I worked at the famous tennis academy in Bradenton, Florida a tall beautiful female pro from America was training there. She represented France when she would play pro tournaments. She was training right before a major tournament. I would run into her a lot on campus after teaching. I asked her out on a date, to go to a disco. She said no because her dad wouldn't like it. If you knew anything about her dad, her dad would have come at me like a nightmare.

NUMBER 5: At Club Green in OKC, Oklahoma they had a female pro tennis tournament every year. One year they had the two beautiful Black sisters playing there. I took a pee in the bathroom next to their dad. I said, "Hey man, how's it going?" and he said, "Good, how are you?" That was it.

NUMBER 6: Another year at the Club Green tournament. The hottest blond female tennis player from Russia. She gave a tennis clinic at Club Quail, while I was working there. I went up to her to say hello. She told her security to kick me out of my own club.

NUMBER 7: Another female pro at the Club Green tournament. I was one of the racquet stringers for the tournament. I had a pass around my neck that would let me go almost anywhere. Years earlier this female pro was stabbed in the back on the court when she was playing in a tournament on a game change by a psychotic German dude. He was obsessed with a German female player back then. At the Club Green tour, I'm with my attorney friend. I told him to wait, and don't go in the stringing room. The female pro and I are talking while I'm stringing her racquet. My friend comes in the room. Because of the stabbing her security team attacks my friend and takes him outside. I just finished her string job. I ran outside and saved my friend's butt. That was a trip.

NUMBER 8: Another female pro at the Club Green tournament. I was working at Club Santa at the time. She was the young pro from New York, New York. When she was younger, she was busted for possession of crack. She was at Club Santa hitting with her hitting partner. I should have asked her to go out with me and smoke crack all night. That was a joke, I'm just trying to be funny. What's sad is, I probably had crack on me at the time.

NUMBER 9: While I was working at Club Santa I put on a couple of clinics with famous playing pros. My favorite clinic was with one of the famous brothers. He and his brother were a great doubles team in the 90's. He was the one who could serve with both arms. We put on a great clinic with a couple of my assistants. I asked him if he would play singles against one of my assistants. My assistant was a national champion college tennis player. And the number one player for Senegal Africa's Davis cup team. Their match was a war with everybody at the clinic watching. My assistant almost got a set off the pro.

NUMBER 10: My encounter with the director of the famous tennis academy in Bradenton, Florida. Before I was leaving at the end of the summer, before I drove home to Oklahoma, I wanted to meet him. I'm in his waiting room about to meet him. He is having a meeting with his top teaching pros. He's yelling at them with furious anger that he's paying them eighteen thousand dollars a year and they suck. After hearing that I didn't want to meet him. I left for Oklahoma City immediately.

Chapter Twenty-Three

2010 Switching Addictions /
Madman Comedy the Frisky and Grumpy Show

Let beer be for those who are perishing, wine for those who are in
anguish.

—Proverbs 31:6

–Big Mess, Devo

Now back to legal drugs are evil. After my girlfriend from Norman
high dumped me I switched addictions from a crack hell to prescription drugs. I joined a 7.0 mixed USTA doubles league. Sweet P, our
female team captain, was a long-time member at Club Santa. That
season my female partner and I never lost. I was so high on all my
pills. I hit the ball as hard as I could and let muscle memory take
over. It's impossible to play tennis on Soma muscle relaxers. Your
muscles have no control. You can't hit a ball in to save your life.

One match on Somas, I couldn't hit a ball in the court. I
never knew what the score was. The team was killing us, then the
muscle relaxers wore off. We won every game, and the match. The
team we were playing was wondering what just happened. That
season we were playing a madwoman and her partner. I'm a nice
guy, but if you mess with me or my partner, I can blow like a nuclear bomb.

In this match we are winning easy. Madwoman starts cheating bad. She and my female partner were fighting like wildcats. Its 105 degrees out and excruciating. We won the first set six to two and it's like four to one in the second. We have been playing in this evil heat for ever. After one point Madwoman cheated, her and my partner argued for ten minutes. During the ten minutes I'm over in the corner kicking a pole. I wanted to scream at Madwoman. Instead, I break my right big toe kicking the pole.

Now we go back to playing. Madwoman starts doing the craziest thing I've ever seen. Her partner hits his serve in. Before I hit his serve, she raises her finger up like she's calling it out. When she sticks her finger up in the air, I didn't swing. I'm confused, then Madwoman says that point is theirs, because I didn't hit the serve back. I tell her you can't stick your finger up in the air before I hit the serve. She says I didn't, what are you talking about and that's our point.

Every serve she did the same thing. Now other people on my team are telling her to stop her madness. This game lasted twenty minutes. I'm overheated and have a broken toe. This match should have been over an hour ago. My partner couldn't get through to her. Now it's my turn.

I told her, quit cheating you're a psychotic freak. She said, how dare you call me that I'm a lady. I said you're not a lady you're coo coo for cocoa puffs. Now her husband comes on the court telling me to chill out. We barked at each other for a while. He went over to talk to his wife. After all this madness the score is still four to one in the second. Madwoman finally stops cheating, we win easy. Thank God the match is finally over. It was a two-hour match in 105 degrees, and the score was six two, six one. It was the most painful match of my life mentally and physically. I'm starting to hate USTA leagues.

I called the husband up and apologized for my behavior a couple days later. He accepted my apology. The next season in 7.0

mixed doubles, we played against Madwoman's husband and his 3.0 partner. Right of the bat he hits me in the chest with a hundred mile an hour forehand. Then he hits my 3.0 female partner with the same. I went nuclear on him and was ready for war. We're on the court acting like two gorillas about to wrestle. He chills out and apologized, then we won. I've been in way too many verbal fights before this one in USTA leagues. After that match. I quit playing USTA leagues for life. Now that I'm writing this book. I am embarrassed about my behavior.

Now it's Craig, Susan, Mary, and myself still alive. Susan and her family moved to Estes's Park, Colorado. They are living in a beautiful house, raising their two children, having a great life. Craig and his family are living in OKC, working for the church. I moved into a one-bedroom upstairs apartment. I called it Upstairs at Erics. I named it after the genius album from the group Yaz. One day, while I'm living in my upstairs apartment, I was in a pill-infused trip and lost my keys. I couldn't get in my apartment and I'm getting frustrated. I go to my car and get a crowbar from the trunk. I snapped and ripped my front door open. The whole time I'm ripping open my door like a gorilla, I didn't realize it. I had new neighbors across the hall freaking out. I was so high all the time and didn't know they moved in. They said they were calling the police. I told them, I lost my keys and they believed me. This whole time my keys were right by my door on the ground.

I was working at my church as a janitor, and a PE instructor for the Christian school at our church. Craig was the principal; my sister-in-law was the head teacher. Being a PE teacher during the day, I wouldn't eat very many of my pills. At night it was black out city.

I want to thank SK, the head pastor at our church, for everything you did for me. If it wasn't for you and the church, I would have died in a crack house somewhere. Pastor K let me live on the church's properties a couple times. The church gave me food and a

job. Everybody in the church gave me incredible love and support. I apologize for all my behavior while I was around everyone at church. Thank you, sincerely Eric Miller. One day at our church, the head pastor told me about a new thing he was starting; Saturday night live at the church to raise money. Every Saturday night, all types of entertainers and acts would get on stage. I told the pastor I'm in and he asked what can I do. I told him standup comedy and I've never done it. He told me he was about to start a program for intercity youth. We need someone to do puppet shows for the kids. He let me do Christian puppet shows at SNL to practice.

I had two days to come up with my first show. I found a cardboard refrigerator box in an alley. I cut the box up and spray painted it. I get behind it and do my show. I called my show the Frisky and Grumpy show. Frisky was a big cat and Grumpy was a tiny dog. They went on adventures spreading the word of Jesus Christ to all the animals in the neighborhood that were hurting inside, like a gang of mean cats that lived under a house, or Sneaky, the gangster badger that was terrorizing the neighborhood animals.

I was on my pills and fearless. The first night of SNL at my Southern Baptist Church I was on after a barber shop quartet. The barber shop quartet was a trip. My pastor introduced me as the Frisky and Grumpy Show by Eric Miller. I didn't know if I was good or bad. One thing I did know, I was hoping I didn't cuss. The microphone I was talking into behind my box was loud. And I was making really wild animal noises. All I know was everybody clapped. From then on, I did it every Saturday.

I took the Frisky and Grumpy show to Children's Hospital. They videotaped it in a little studio. I did my first episode of the Frisky and Grumpy show. They told me they were going to show my video for the sick children in their rooms. I was so high all the time. I don't know if they played it for the kids. That would be cool having the video of the show.

I went and got my street entertainer's license so I could legally do standup and puppet shows on the street. In an arts district in OKC, I would go outside with a tip bucket, wait for some people to walk by, then start doing standup without a microphone. Imagine you're walking through a beautiful arts district and there's a madman yelling out standup comedy. People would be waiting for a punch line or the point. My comedy is absurd and manic. I think they felt sorry for me and gave me a little bit of money. I thought I was a pro and was going to make a living at comedy. I didn't make enough money to buy a pizza the whole week of my comedy career. Crowds in the arts district in OKC are tough.

I got cocky and decided to go to an open mic night at the biggest comedy club in OKC. My first try at stand up with a lot of people. And they paid money to come watch us perform. Before the show I took a bunch of pills. I was wearing my Misfits t-shirt and overalls. I was so high I forgot I was there. All the sudden I hear the MC say, "For the first time ever Eric Miller." I wake up and walk on stage. I look at the big crowd and I was blinded by

the stage light. I forgot everything I worked on. I started singing House of Pain's song, "Jump Around."

The MC made fun of me. I started messing with the MC on the mic. He told me to leave the club. I told him to come make me leave. He was a big ole boy, then he put his mic down. He came at me, and I flew out the side door. My first and only big standup comedy act was being run out the club. This is a joke I wrote lately. When I tell my jokes I also act them out.

427 Jets Joke: One day, there was this fat cocky kid, walking down the street singing opera. He sees a one-eyed cat peeping in a sea food store with laser focus. The fat cocky kid kicks the cat. The cat goes flying. The cat comes back and tears the kid up. When this kid is scared, he farts a lot. So, the kid is on the ground (*fart, fart*) saying, "Why cat did you (*fart, fart*) hurt me so bad (*fart, fart*)?"

The one-eyed cat says, "Because I'm a one-eyed cat fool." The end. After all my pill blackout insanity I went to get help.

Chapter Twenty-Four

2015 Suboxone Drug Treatment in OKC, Oklahoma /
Mary Miller Dies

For I consider that the sufferings of this present time are not worth comparing with the glory that is to be revealed to us.

—Romans 8:18

–Burning Inside, Ministry

I went to a Suboxone clinic in OKC for help. Suboxone blocks the effects from opioids. There's no point in taking opioid painkillers if you can't get high. I worked the program hard and stayed sober. I had to take random drug tests. I had therapy with my doctor in charge of the program. I had to go to a certain number of Alcoholics Anonymous meetings a week. I had to get a paper signed by the group chairperson. Jennifer and my AA home group was the Classen Club in OKC.

Dealing with self-destruction for most my life was hard. I was so alone and angry as hell, for wasting my life. Like not having money, wife, kids, house, car, and security. I had nothing. I did have the most important thing in my life. I came back to God. God never leaves us, we leave God. I was still doing puppet shows at my church and sober. I got a lot better at doing puppet shows. The new intercity kids' program at our church was every Saturday. We

MARY 1981
17

were giving the kids fun bible education with Christian puppet shows, arts, crafts, singing, delicious lunch, and more. Suboxone worked and God was back in my life.

My mother Mary was diagnosed with colon cancer and started chemotherapy. It was a terrible time; we didn't get along. I was trying to take care of her. I was with her every day all night long. Mary was getting worse from her cancer fast. I was doing things for her. Like helping her go to the bathroom and changing her diapers. Thank God I was on Suboxone, or I would have been taking Mary's painkillers. Mary was getting a lot of high fevers. I was calling an ambulance constantly. I finally had to admit her to the hospital.

Mary had colin cancer, but she died of a stroke. During her stroke I was in her hospital room. She started screaming bloody murder in pain. She stood up on her bed, it was very creepy. It was like something out of the exorcist movie. I called for the nurses, and they put her out with meds. Mary had a massive stroke; she was a vegetable. The doctor said, Mary wasn't coming out of her coma. Susan, Craig, and I took her off oxygen. Then Mary Miller died. After a lifetime of mental pain, she was finally out of her misery. What I'm getting at is rape is murder. Both Jennifer and Mary's lives were destroyed from being raped. They didn't have a chance in hell of being happy. I'm extremely pissed off right now thinking about it.

Right before Mary was diagnosed with cancer, we were hanging out a lot. One day I asked her why she didn't like me. She said, I don't like you because you remind me of me. That was chilling, and confusing. She apologized for it, and I forgave her. I apologized to Mary, for being such a crazy drug addict my whole life.

I turned into a sugar addict. There's a lot of sugar in alcohol. When you quit drinking you crave sugar. When alcoholics and drug addicts stop using they tend to go to the next thing that gives them pleasure. I gained forty pounds quick, now chocolate is my new addiction.

At the time. I was talking to my older sister Susan. She told me to come down to visit Estes Park, Colorado. I went down there for a week. There was no crime and ghettos. There weren't any crack houses, prostitutes walking down the street, and gun fights. I was in culture shock, and it was a great one. The mountains are massive, and the town is beautiful. I was sober for a long time in the Suboxone program. I was tired of OKC, because of what I made from it.

Susan asked me, if I wanted to move to Estes Park, Colorado. I did it without a second thought. Susan and Cool Dude bought a two-bedroom condo in Estes Park. They let me rent it for OKC ghetto prices. Goodbye Oklahoma, I'll be back one of these days.

Chapter Twenty-Five

2017 Estes Park, Colorado / Summer in Jail

Please God don't let anything bad happen to me in jail.
—Eric Miller, scared and praying

–Fun to Be Had, Nitzer Ebb

I was on Suboxone for opioid addiction. Moving to Estes Park meant I had to get off it. My doctor in OKC told me to taper off, you'll be just fine. My doctor was full of crap! I spent ten days with withdrawals from hell. I didn't sleep for ten days and had the opioid kicks. I was screaming into my pillow with chest pains. It was the worst withdrawals I've ever had. I could have died; I should have been in a detox hospital.

After that horrible experience my chronic strep throat came back that I have had for years in Oklahoma. Thank God, I got Medicaid from Colorado. I could finally get a tonsillectomy for my strep. The pain from recovering from my tonsillectomy was insane. I became weak with my sobriety. I started drinking alcohol again.

I found a karaoke bar in Estes Park. It was perfect for my craving attention. I turned into a fat cocky drunk with a micro-phone. At karaoke, I was singing anything from Depeche Mode to The Diamonds. One night after karaoke, I drank and drove home.

Left to right: Cool Dude, me, and my sister Susan on Halloween.

I was pulled over by the Estes Park police. I got my third DUI, and your third DUI is bad. I went to court. They gave me three months in work release jail in Fort Collins, Colorado. My jail time was in the summer. In work release jail you're supposed to have a job. You go back and forth to work and jail every day. I took a chance and called up a big-time tennis school in Fort Collins. LL is the boss and owns the tennis school. I was trying to teach there for the summer. LL wanted to see me teach with his junior program first. He liked what he saw and hired me. My new boss LL is the best director of tennis in Colorado. He is also a minister, owns a music recording studio, and is a professional musician. He has a big-time junior tennis program. It's better than anything I've ever made.

I loved teaching tennis again, but it was hard. I had to ride a bicycle back and forth to work and jail. I was riding a bicycle all over Fort Collins, about ten or more miles a day. I was teaching about ten hours a day. I was 240 pounds and hadn't exercised in years. Jail was scary for a while. Then I realized, most dudes were in there for DUI and drug charges. Just like me, we all had something in common.

There wasn't any violence, because nobody wanted more time. I lived in dorms in jail with six bunk beds with twelve wild dudes in my dorm. I had to sleep on the top bunk that was made of metal. One of the first nights on the top bunk, I fell to the ground hard in a dead sleep. My dorm mates were mostly Mexicans. I felt like I was in a nice Mexican gang.

Every day you had to check out with the staff for work. Then you had to get back to jail on time or you got written up. Everybody had chores to do every day. If you were written up, they gave you more chores or worse.

We had to take random piss tests called UAs. This could tell if you were drinking days before or using drugs. If you tested positive you were screwed. Once a week somebody would break a law in jail. Then the staff would call for lock down. Everybody had to go to their rooms and stand by their bed. The police were coming to take someone to real jail. Meaning, you were going to be locked in a tiny cell with a bunch of violent greasy dudes. It would have been for the rest of your sentence. I made sure I didn't get in trouble for anything. Work release jail was a luxurious resort compared to jail.

One day they called lock down. There was a dude in my dorm, his name was Eric. Everybody called him by a nickname. I didn't know that at the time. Two police came in our dorm room. The police said, "Eric, put your hands behind your back." I freaked out and said, what did I do. The police weren't talking to me. They were talking to the other Eric and took him to real jail.

One day in jail the Mad Pooper struck. The Mad Pooper put a big juicy turd right by the front desk staff. The staff called for lock down. The staff was questioning dudes if they knew who the Mad Pooper was. It was glorious because we were all so bored. They couldn't catch the Mad Pooper. He was out of camera view. A couple days later the Mad Pooper struck again. He put a big juicy turd between one of the couch seats. Some dude put his hand in the couch and found the turd.

They called lock down again and tried to find the Mad Pooper. They never caught the Mad Pooper, he was genius. At LL tennis school in Fort Collins, there was a great teaching pro from California. Cool Cali loves the band The Cult. LL would let me bring his ghetto blaster on the court. For the junior program, I got to play whatever I wanted. That's trouble.

The junior program was listening to The Cramps, Devo, D-Mode, The Cult, The Misfits, and Link Wray. Cool Cali and I would start at eight AM. We would teach every age group. Around four PM, we taught the top juniors group. They were some of the best junior tennis players in Colorado. Then I would teach the adult classes. I would ride five miles back to jail in the dark. I would hang out with my jail buddies. Then I would wake up real early and do it again.

I must thank the director of tennis, LL, for hiring me. No one would have given a dude in jail a chance. The summer tennis and jail ended. LL wanted me to move to Fort Collins, and work for him. I went back to Estes Park where my probation was. My probation was worse than jail. I had a ton of DUI classes, UAs, community service, Mothers Against Drunk Driving class, and more.

I spend all my money on probation and couldn't pay my sister rent. She gave me a million breaks, or I would have been homeless in paradise. My probation is for two and a half years. I would rather have spent a year in jail instead of probation. DUIs are no joke. All this crap from my DUI, is my doing. I have learned that I do not want a fourth DUI. It is a felony and two years in jail or worse. What if I kill a family from driving drunk? I can't comprehend how bad that would be.

From my third DUI, the number one thing that I have learned is that the only way I am not getting another DUI is to never drink again, because I cannot control my drinking.

Chapter Twenty-Six

2018 to 2021 Estes Park Colorado a Test from God

*God, Grant me the serenity to accept the things I cannot change,
the courage to change the things I can, and the wisdom to know
the difference.*

—The Alcoholics Anonymous Serenity Prayer

–Do it Clean, Echo and the Bunnymen

I told you about withdrawing, tonsillectomy and jail. Now winter
is kicking in. Estes Park has crazy cold winters. It has below zero
temperatures with strong winds. My driver's license is suspended.
I'm walking to my job every day.

No matter how warm I dressed I felt like I was climbing
Mount Everest, walking around Estes Park. The elk will attack you
and possibly kill you. I'm constantly running into hundreds of
angry elk. I'm in a war zone and the elk are the king warriors. During this test from God, I'm cussing God out. The winters here are
painful and the wind makes me furious.

When spring showed up I found people to play tennis with.
We started playing a lot of doubles. Estes Park has good tennis
players. That summer I was playing good tennis again. I was riding
my bicycle everywhere and getting in shape. Estes Park tennis
community, I love you.

I was talking to my therapist Cool Casey at Summit Stone Mental Health in Estes Park. Cool Casey tells me about a shot called Vivitrol. It blocks the effects of alcohol. It might help me to stop drinking. I committed to the Vivitrol shot once a month. I made an appointment to get my first Vivitrol shot. On the day of my first shot, I was late for my appointment.

I was riding my bicycle on the wrong side of the road. I was going forty miles per hour down a long hill. I was on the shoulder, then a car pulled in front of me. I veered out of the way and flew into a ditch of rocks. I pulled an Evil Knievel and woke up in an ambulance. They were taking me to the Estes Park hospital. The paramedic in the ambulance told me I flew fifty feet. I hit every big rock like a rag doll. I wasn't wearing a helmet.

I had a broken right collar bone and a bunch of broken ribs. My broken ribs punctured my right lung and it collapsed. I had the worst concussion I've ever had. The ER doctor at Estes Park hospital put a chest tube in my collapsed lung. Then they rushed me to another hospital down the valley to have surgery on my collar bone. They put a metal plate with screws on my collar bone. I was in a hospital in Fort Collins to heal. I was on a ton of pain meds and still crying in pain. The doctors and nurses told me that I should have died. They really let me have it for not wearing a helmet. My head not exploding, or brain damage is a miracle from God. Obviously, God has a purpose for me. When God reveals it to me, I'm going all out with it.

In the hospital the doctor's found cancer in both my kidneys. They're going to cut the cancer out of my left kidney first. My bones need to heal some before they operate. I'm on painkillers and muscle relaxers again in my life. I'm lying in bed miserable in pain for six weeks. I'm sleeping sitting up and can't move. I'm addicted to opioid painkillers again.

My kidney operation was in September. They cut out a fourth of my left kidney. Now I'm at home still recovering from broken bones. I also have five holes in my gut from my kidney operation. I have another catheter jammed up my urethra, peeing into a bag. I'm wanting to give up again on life.

My surgeon told me the mass in my left kidney wasn't cancer. There's still cancer in my right kidney. I can't worry about that right now. I quit cussing God out and started praying. I healed from all my physical pain. Now it's time to attack my mental pain. In the last couple years, I've had good periods of sobriety and relapses. It was time to try to fix that serious problem. I committed to the Vivitrol shot again. I'm not going to die trying to make it to my appointment.

I took my first Vivitrol shot in the butt cheek. I had to see for myself if it really blocked the effects of alcohol. I went to the local bar one day. I started drinking beer and taking shots of Tequila. I drank really hard and fast. After a few beers and shots, zero buzz. I'm freaking out thinking this Vivitrol shot is working. I had to make sure, so I drank a few more beers and shots. I'm on the back patio at the bar with zero buzz. I'm talking to a total stranger, and puke on his shoes. I fall on the ground, and I felt paralyzed. The best part was, I have zero buzz. Thank God the Vivitrol shot works. The manager of the bar told me to leave and she's calling the police. Thank God some nice ladies helped me to their car. They took me home. Because of my puke reign of terror on the crowded patio I was banned from that bar for life.

I finally wanted sobriety more than my life itself. When I got a good chunk of sobriety I saw how great life gets quick. I tried everything for most my life to get sober. It finally came down to jail, suicidal thoughts, and hating myself. When I took my first Vivitrol shot I also went to a psychiatrist. I talked to him about Ritalin for my ADHD. I've been on Ritalin for a while now. I've been working on my book since 2005. Because of sobriety and Ritalin, I have finished my book in the last two years. My family is very pleased with me for the first time in a long time.

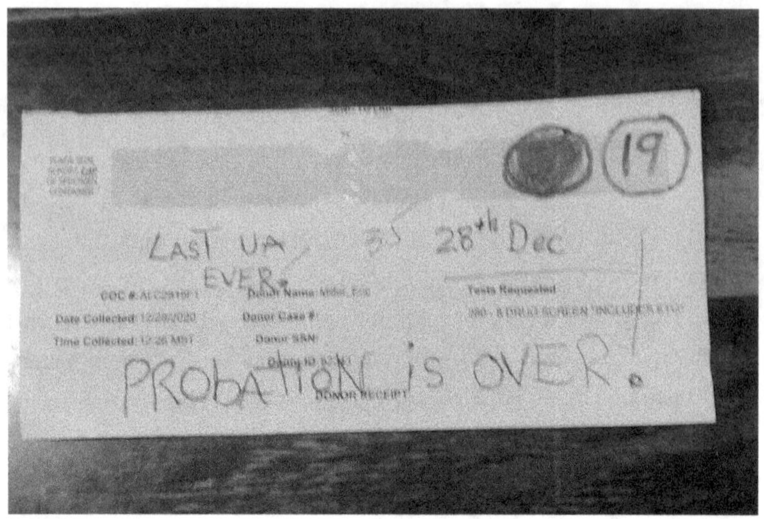

Cool Casey asked me if I would speak at a drug overdose awareness day at an amphitheater in the mountains in Estes Park. I went on stage and spoke on my life of chemical dependency. I talked about my sister Jennifer's drug overdoses and death. I'm ready for God's purpose in my life. I'm ready to stop being selfish and work for God. That's all I want. Special thanks! Thank you, Cool Casey and George at Summit Stone. Thank you, Susan and Cool Dude for being there. Thank you, Craig for being there. Thank you, Kurt at UC Timberline. Thank you, Jill B. for being there. Thank you, Marcelo for being my attorney for my book. Thank you, Aussie OKC for putting up with me all these years. Everything is not even close to being great in my life. Half my life I've been a miserable crazy person. I'm starting to learn how to love myself and stop the negative self-talk. God is a loving God; God will never give up on you. I'm not getting cocky thinking I am cured for life. Writing this book is a constant reminder. I don't care if this book ever sells. I had to finish it for my therapy. God has forgiven me for my wasted life. I need to forgive myself. I'm finally back to where I was before my first drink in 1982. Now it's time to grow up!

THE END

"I Haven't Been Myself Lately," by John Reuben
The lyrics to this song are exactly how I feel about my life. It's time
for change and I can't do it without you God.

www.ingramcontent.com/pod-product-compliance
Lightning Source LLC
Chambersburg PA
CBHW052038150726
48002CB00002B/657